Storybook Talk

Conversations for Comprehension

*Mary Hohmann and
Kate Adams*

HIGHSCOPE PRESS ®

Ypsilanti, Michigan

PUBLISHED BY

HIGHSCOPE® PRESS
A division of the
HIGHSCOPE EDUCATIONAL RESEARCH FOUNDATION
600 NORTH RIVER STREET
YPSILANTI, MICHIGAN 48198-2898
734.485.2000, FAX 734.485.0704
press@highscope.org
highscope.org

Editor: Jennifer Burd, HighScope Press
Cover design, text design, production: Judy Seling, Seling Design
Cover illustration: Robin Ward
Photography:
Patricia Evans — 35
HighScope staff — 9, 41
Gregory Fox — All other photos

Library of Congress Cataloging-in-Publication Data
Hohmann, Mary.
  Storybook talk : conversations for comprehension / Mary Hohmann and Kate Adams.
    p. cm.
  ISBN 978-1-57379-353-7 (soft cover : alk. paper) 1. Reading comprehension. 2. Children--Books and reading. 3. Interaction analysis in education. I. Adams, Kate. II. Title.
  LB1050.45.H64 2008
  372.47--dc22
                                    2008005017

Printed in the United States of America
10 9 8 7 6 5 4 3 2

Storybook Talk

Conversations for
Comprehension

Contents

Preface

Intuitively, we know that comprehension skills should be a major predictor of young children's future reading success. However, there is little to no research to support this notion (NELP, 2006). Alphabet knowledge and phonological awareness continue to be heralded as the best-known predictors of effective readers (Lonigan et al., 2000). It is not easy to do comprehension research studies with prereaders due to lack of reliable and valid assessments. That is the main reason we have little empirical evidence to support this skill as a predictor. Does this mean that a focus on comprehension skill development is unimportant? Certainly not!

There is an abundance of studies on young children's vocabulary development (Beck et al., 2002; Biemiller, 2006; Senechel & Cornell, 1993; Richman & Columbo, 2007). It is not as difficult to measure growth in this area due to the common use of the Peabody Picture Vocabulary Test (PPVT), a test that some would argue is culturally biased (Dunn & Dunn, 1997). Many make the mistake of using this and other vocabulary instruments as a measure of comprehension, ignoring the need to measure more age-appropriate discrete skills in this area, such as connection to life, prediction, and retelling (DeBruin-Parecki, 2008). Although we know that a large bank of vocabulary words is necessary for expression of complex ideas, it is not the only piece vital to children's gaining of understanding. Some would argue that children begin comprehending at birth before formal language (Snow, 2001). We need to teach vocabulary and comprehension skills side by side, not one at the expense of the other.

So how do we teach these skills in ways that make sense to young children? The answer is to teach them in authentic contexts such as storybook reading and everyday conversation. Research shows that teaching children comprehension strategies during interactive book reading can lead to improvement in understanding over time (Bus et al., 1995; DeBruin-Parecki, 2007, 2007a; Sonnenschein & Munsterman, 2002). Authentic contexts for instruction, and in turn for assessment, can assist researchers in completing necessary studies to show the value of comprehension skills as a predictor for successful reading.

The Early Literacy Skills Assessment (ELSA) is a reliable and valid tool that successfully measures a variety of comprehension skills within the authentic context of interactive one-on-one storybook reading (DeBruin-Parecki, 2004, 2005). This assessment is typically used in formal settings such as preschools with children aged 2½–6. The Adult/Child Interactive Reading Inventory (ACIRI; DeBruin-Parecki, 2007), another reliable and valid tool, measures comprehension skills while observing an adult and a child aged 2½–6 years reading together. This tool is used primarily in family literacy and parent programs. In the case of both pre/post instruments, results provide teachers with needed information to individualize literacy instruction and to enhance the teaching of comprehension skills. We need more authentic tools such as these to provide accurate data for studies and to assist teachers with curriculum design. We also need progress monitoring tools so teachers can do "quick checks" to see how children are improving over time.

Zimmerman and Hutchins (2003, pp. 6–7) in their book *7 Keys to Comprehension* recommend the following to increase children's reading comprehension skills:

1. Create mental images
2. Use background knowledge
3. Ask questions
4. Make inferences
5. Determine important ideas or themes
6. Synthesize information
7. Use fix-up strategies such as rereading

While their book is aimed at helping young readers, their seven keys work equally well for prereaders with the assistance of an adult. All of their research-based seven keys have appeared somewhere in this book along with additional valuable and theoretically sound strategies for using interactive book reading and conversation to promote comprehension.

The authors of *Storybook Talk* have provided the reader with a wide variety of methods for enhancing prereaders' comprehension skills. The book is filled with research-based strategies that will assist teachers in promoting comprehension within activity-based small groups, read-alouds, and during classroom conversations. In addition, suggestions for books linked to specific skill development are provided. Parents and caregivers will also find this book useful, as it gives clear, practical examples of when and how to use comprehension strategies in conversations and during book reading. In summary, this well-researched book will act as a most needed resource for those who seek to scaffold children into becoming not just decoders but motivated readers who understand what they are reading and who can transfer knowledge gained to a variety of contexts.

Andrea DeBruin-Parecki, Ph.D.
Old Dominion University

References

Beck, I. L., McKeown, M. G., & Kucan, L. (2002). *Bringing words to life: Robust vocabulary instruction.* New York: Guilford Press.

Biemiller. A. (2006). Vocabulary development and instruction: A perspective for school learning. In D. K. Dickinson & S. B. Neuman (Eds.), *Handbook of early literacy research: Vol. 2* (pp. 41–51). New York: Guilford Press.

Bus, A. J., van Ijzendoorn, M. H., & Pellegrini, A. D. (1995). Joint book reading makes for success in learning to read: A meta-analysis on intergenerational transmission of literacy. *Review of Educational Research, 65*(1), 1–21.

DeBruin-Parecki, A. (2004). *The Early Literacy Skills Assessment (ELSA): Violet's adventure/La aventura de Violet.* Ypsilanti, MI: High/Scope Press.

DeBruin-Parecki, A. (2005). *The Early Literacy Skills Assessment (ELSA): Dante grows up/El cambio en Dante.* Ypsilanti, MI: High/Scope Press.

DeBruin-Parecki, A. (2007). *Let's read together: Improving literacy outcomes with the adult/child interactive reading inventory.* Brookes Publishing Company: Baltimore, MD.

DeBruin-Parecki, A. (April 2007a). *Assessment of early literacy skills through storybook reading.* Paper presented at the annual meeting of the American Educational Research Association: Chicago, Illinois.

DeBruin-Parecki, A. (2008). Storybook reading as a standardized measurement of early literacy skill development. In author (Ed.), *Effective early literacy in practice: Here's how, here's why.* Baltimore, MD: Brookes Publishing Company.

Dunn, L. M., & Dunn, L. M. (1997). *Peabody Picture Vocabulary Test-III.* Circle Pines, MN: American Guidance Service.

Lonigan, C. J., S. R. Burgess, et al. (2000). Development of emergent literacy and early reading skills in preschool children: Evidence from a latent-variable longitudinal study. *Developmental Psychology 36*(5): 596–613.

National Early Literacy Panel (NELP; March 2006). *Findings from the National Early Literacy Panel: Providing a focus for early language and literacy development.* Presented at the meeting of the National Center for Family Literacy: Louisville, KY.

Richman, W. A., & Colombo, J. (2007). Joint book reading in the second year and vocabulary outcomes. *Journal of Research in Childhood Education, 21*(3), 242–253.

Senechal, M., & Cornell, E. H. (1993). Vocabulary acquisition through shared reading experiences. *Reading Research Quarterly, 28,* 361–374.

Snow, C. E. (2001). Knowing what we know: Children, teachers, researchers. *Educational Researcher, 30*(7): 3–9.

Sonnenschein, S., & Munsterman, K. (2002). The influence of home-based reading interactions on 5-year olds' reading motivations and early literacy development. *Early Childhood Research Quarterly, 17*(3), 318–337.

Zimmerman, S., & Hutchins, C. (2003). *7 keys to comprehension: How to help your kids read it and get it.* New York: Three Rivers Press.

Storybook Talk

Conversations for
Comprehension

1
How "Story Talk" Builds Comprehension and Oral Language

Settling into your lap with *Caps for Sale* (Slobodkina), Pat says, "Let's read the funny monkey story again!" You've read "the funny monkey story" countless times this week and it's only Tuesday! You wonder how you can maintain your enthusiasm for the plight of the peddler who loses his caps to a tree full of monkeys.

Well, wonder no more! This book offers ways to make reading a beloved book over and over again with children as engaging and compelling for you as it is for the children. The strategies offered will (1) change what you and the children see in a book's illustrations and understand about the story itself and (2) shape the discussions you have with each interactive reading. Even though the storybook remains the same, you and the children can focus on different aspects of the story each time you read.

Story Conversations Play a Critical Role

Listening to stories puts children in touch with story structure, literacy conventions, grammatical structures, and story language they will need to understand written text (Cochran-Smith, 1984; Bus, van Ijzendoon, & Pellegrini, 1995). But simply listening to stories is not enough. We know from years of reading research (Teale, 2003) that reading aloud with children in a way that engages them in thought and dialogue is essential to building the story comprehension and expressive language that motivates children to read and enables them to learn from reading.

When psychologists and reading researchers Margaret McKeown and Isabel Beck (2006) asked themselves what about reading aloud promotes story comprehension and literacy development, they took another look at existing research. Here is what they found.

Reading the same book many times never loses its appeal when you focus on a different aspect of the story each time you and the children read it together.

Thoughtful story talk promotes language development. Talk during storybook reading that gets children to think about what is going on in the story is the most valuable aspect of reading aloud for enhancing children's language development (Snow, Tabors, Nicholson, & Kurland, 1995).

Dialogue during reading promotes comprehension and vocabulary. The way this "talk surrounding the text" (Morrow, 1992) occurs makes a difference. Story talk has the most positive effects on children's story comprehension (and vocabulary) when it occurs *during* storybook reading, involves both children and the adult, and engages children in thinking about story content or language (Dickinson & Smith, 1994).

Just reading a story aloud to children with no child-adult talk during reading is the *least* effective way to build children's vocabulary and story comprehension, while the interactive, child-teacher dialogue style of reading is the *most* effective way (Brabham & Lynch-Brown, 2002).

Awareness of story episodes influences retelling. After hearing and discussing a story, children retell more fully if the adult has drawn their attention to and elicited children's talk about story parts or episodes during story reading (Teale & Martinez, 1996).

Time to think encourages conversation. The most effective way to encourage child talk about important story ideas is to give children time to think and then speak, rather than supplying answers for children who do not speak up quickly (Teale & Martinez, 1996).

Storytelling skills develop. Conversational reading (also referred to as dialogic or interactive reading) encourages children to become storytellers over time (Whitehurst et al., 1988; Sulzby, 1985).

A shared story focus builds conversational coherence. The amount of reciprocal, turn-taking conversation between adults and children relates profoundly to children's verbal and cognitive competence, mainly because each person must say something related to the shared topic. With time and practice, children learn to sort, select, and construct responses that allow a coherent conversation to continue (Hart & Risley, 1999).

How This Book Is Organized

Chapter 1 of *Storybook Talk: Conversations for Comprehension* is the "why story talk matters" chapter. It makes the case for interactive talk during story reading by showing how story talk fosters children's comprehension and ability to express what they understand about story characters, actions, and ideas.

Chapter 2 is the "homework" chapter. It guides you through story selection and analysis so *you* know what kinds of stories support comprehension development and how these stories work before reading them with children. The chapter includes a listing of narrative storybooks, Mother Goose books, and rhyming stories to read with children, including books mentioned in examples throughout the rest of this book.

Chapter 3 is the "get started" chapter. It offers strategies that promote child talk for you to use *each time* you sit down with children and a book.

Chapters 4 through 7 are the "let's keep this interesting" chapters. They give strategies for varying the storybook conversations you have with children so, for example, you can read *Caps for Sale* with enjoyment 50 times or more, each time with a slightly different focus — on vocabulary (Chapter 4), making connections to and across the story (Chapter 5), retelling story episodes (Chapter 6), or predicting what lies ahead (Chapter 7).

Note that the teaching strategies presented in this book are numbered sequentially, beginning in Chapter 3 and continuing through Chapter 7.

The appendix at the end of this book contains a master list of all the strategies given in Chapters 3–7.

Preschool Readers in Action

Let's listen in on a group of young readers as they read *Rosie's Walk* (Hutchins), a virtually wordless book in which Rosie the hen takes a walk around the farm while a fox sneaks after her, pouncing at every chance.

"I see … um, a … fox!" *(Points to fox)*

"Tongue. His tongue out like this." *(Demonstrates)*

"He's hiding under … under the house."

Since dialogue plays a critical role during storybook reading, giving a child time to think and speak is essential.

"Hey, that her house!"

"Yeh, Rosie's house. He hidin' under there."

"Uh-oh. He gonna get her!"

Hovering over the first two pages of the book, these preschool children think about the pictures and express, in gestures and words, what they understand about them. As they gather factual information about characters and setting and — based on what they see — make some interpretations about what the fox is doing and why, they are building *comprehension* strategies they will need later on when they learn to read and make sense of written text.

To read, children need to be able to recognize and sound out words. To be *motivated* to read and learn through reading, they need to see it as a source of both information and pleasure. To view reading in these ways, children need to engage with text, make sense of it, and connect events and ideas into a coherent story or line of thought. And that's exactly what the children in the above example are doing! Conversation during story reading helps children build the comprehension strategies they need, as emergent readers and later as accomplished readers, for the rest of their lives. So, what is comprehension, and why is it important for preschoolers?

Story Comprehension

Comprehension is the process of *making meaning* of the objects, events, interactions, speech, and text one encounters in everyday life and understanding the connections and relationships among sets of people, actions, words, and ideas. From birth onward, people make meaning by fitting new information into what they already know. This often involves forming new mental structures that alter what they currently see, think, and understand (Anderson & Pearson, 1984).

One specific part of comprehension is *narrative or story comprehension,* the process of making sense of stories represented in pictures and spoken or written words. This is a complex mental undertaking for readers of all ages, especially for young children who need to hear and see and think about lots of stories again and again just to begin to understand how stories work in general and what specific stories mean to them.

Children enjoy listening to stories so much that we may not realize how much effort it requires. The hard work of story comprehension involves the *recognition* and *recall* of story characters and events as well as the more complex *integrative thinking* required to actively construct meaning (Paris & Paris, 2003). To weave a series of events into a single, coherent narrative, children have to hold in mind multiple aspects of the story. This requires more "brain power" than thinking about a single character or event.

Children find meaning in stories through the *active, minds-on* process of examining and thinking about story characters and events and working to put these thoughts into words. Accustomed as we are to promoting children's active engagement with people, materials, and physical action, we often focus primarily on the tangible, physical aspects of books; for example, how to hold them, what's on the cover, how to turn the pages, the difference between pictures and words, and book-related props. However, we also need to support children's active mental engagement with the story itself, whose characters and episodes come to life only through the efforts of the mind.

To understand story narratives, in addition to engaging with the story, children also need to *gather information* and use what they know to *make inferences.* Psychologists and reading researchers Alison Paris and Scott Paris describe the reader's need for both explicit information and implicit information (Paris & Paris, 2001). Gathering explicit information about a story includes figuring out who the characters are, where the story takes place, what the problem is that drives the story along, what starts the problem, and how it gets resolved. This information is clearly shown in the pictures and/or stated in the text.

A more complex level of thinking is required for young children to figure out *implied meaning,* that is, meaning that is not stated directly through pictures and words but is suggested by them. A story, for example, may suggest or give clues about what characters are feeling, what they intend to do next, how events happen, why characters act as they do, and what overarching idea ties the whole story together. *Rosie's Walk* explicitly begins with the words "Rosie the hen went for a walk" and shows Rosie the hen walking along in each picture. Additionally, because Rosie strikes

Children of all ages love to look at, listen to, and talk about stories with adults who themselves take pleasure in books.

virtually the same straight-ahead pose and facial expression in each picture, it is possible to *infer* from the whole set of pictures that Rosie is either unaware of the fox, is hard of hearing, is unconcerned for her safety, or understands that the fox is not really clever enough to catch her. So, as you can see, identifying the character Rosie the hen, and figuring out how she feels about her situation, are two different types of information a preschooler needs to grapple with in order to make sense of this "simple" virtually wordless picture book!

How Children Develop the Ability to Think About Stories

To put the process of story comprehension in perspective, it may help to remember that learning the names of 26 alphabet letters and the 50-plus sounds they represent is a finite task generally mastered by the age of eight. Learning to comprehend stories, on the other hand, is a thought process that begins in preschool and continues into adulthood as one encounters stories of increasing depth and narrative complexity.

Although we cannot peer inside children's heads to see their thoughts about stories, *we can engage them in thought-provoking conversations* about stories and listen to them carefully to gauge how they think about and understand stories. From the pioneering early comprehension assessment work of Paris (Paris & Paris, 2001; Paris & Paris, 2003) and reading researcher Elizabeth Sulzby (Sulzby, 1985; Sulzby & Barnhart, 1990; Sulzby & Rockafellow, 2001), we have an idea about how narrative comprehension develops in preschool children, which is briefly summarized here.

Children progress from making isolated comments to making connected comments about stories. Preschool children are most likely to make comments about the one picture and story event they are seeing or hearing about at the moment: "There's a nest … in the tree!" "She's walking." With support and experience, they move toward making comments that connect one picture or episode to the next: "He's jumping at Rosie *(turns the page)* … He gets on the rake! He doesn't get Rosie."

Children progress from identifying explicit story details to making inferences. It is easier for preschool children to identify and recount specific information that is clearly stated in the pictures or text of the story, information such as who the characters are and what is happening in a particular picture or episode; for example, "That's the hen" or "He's falling in the water!" Gradually, children begin to understand and talk about aspects of the story that are *suggested* by the pictures and words: "Now he looks … he looks scared."

Children progress from a focus on the present to recalling the past and imagining the future. Preschool children begin talking about storybooks using verbs that are "typically present tense, present progressive, or odd uses like *gonna,* which appears to characterize the presently-pictured action" (Sulzby, 1985, p. 466). For example, a child might say, "There goes the wagon! Fox gonna go with it." As they develop a more coherent sense of story, children begin to use the past- and future-tense verbs to refer to parts of the story that have already happened ("He tried … and then … then that stuff … it felled on him!") and to forecast upcoming episodes ("That pile … it might stop him").

Children progress from everyday conversational language to storybook language. Preschool children generally talk about and read storybooks in a conversational manner, pointing to objects and characters and making observations and comments about what they see on the page. They and their listeners need to see the pictures to make sense of what the child is saying: "Uh-oh, boink on the nose!" says a child, pointing to the picture of the fox getting hit in the nose by the rake. Gradually, children begin to add to their speech "parts that sound like written language, either in intonation or wording or both" (Sulzby, 1985, p. 469). That is, the language they use itself carries more of the story and is less dependent on the accompanying illustration. For example, when a child says "Uh-oh, the rake hits the fox 'boink' on the nose!" his words provide enough information for you to form a mental image of the situation without referring to the illustration.

▼

So, story comprehension develops gradually in preschool children as they examine and think about story details and attempt to connect what they know and understand into coherent speech that moves away from just the here-and-now to include the past and the future.

Therefore, children find repeated readings of "the funny monkey" story, *Rosie's Walk,* or any other storybook both compelling and necessary. Over a course of readings, as they discuss what they see and hear and what tickles or puzzles them about a story character or situation, they develop the habit of working out how a story works and what it means.

2

Story Selection and Analysis: "I Love This Book!"

A three-year-old has a wonderful talent for just looking! Watch him as he looks at a favorite picture-book, turning a page rarely, and gazing with complete absorption at pictures already familiar. His eyes travel appreciatively from one detail to another, and when he moves on to the next picture there is satisfaction in every line of his relaxed little body (Duff, p. 95).

Children have the capacity for "just looking" and losing themselves in pictures and stories as long as we supply them with books that engage their thought and imagination.

How do we select such books for children? We do so by considering their illustrations, words, "worlds," and story structure. Let's take a look at each of these selection criteria.

Illustrations

For most preschool children, reading is picture reading — so for them, the illustrations in books tell as much of the story as the text, and often even more. Wordless books, in fact, rely completely on pictures to tell the story.

This child is absorbed in a book. The pictures engage her completely.

As you build a children's book collection, include books illustrated by a range of artists so that your collection offers children a visual feast in a variety of media including, for example, pen and ink, oils, water colors, and collage. Include books with simple pictures, books with detailed full-page and two-page spreads, and books like *Night Noises* (Fox) with several inset drawings per page. Make sure colors vary from black and white, as seen in the line drawings in *The Story of Ferdinand* (Leaf), to shades of red, orange, yellow, and green, as in *Rosie's Walk* (Hutchins), to a full pallette of colors like those in *Mother Goose* (Long). Supplied with drawing and painting styles that vary from illustrator to illustrator, children see the world rendered from many human perspectives. Additionally, they gain visual awareness of design features, graphic styles, and drawing techniques. For children learning English as another language, illustrations provide a stable set of objects and actions to look at and talk about in their own language and opportunities to connect new words in either language with vivid representations.

For most preschool children, reading is picture reading, and with books illustrated by a wide range of artists, children can see the world rendered from many human perspectives.

Well-illustrated stories continually surprise their readers. The more time you spend looking at them, the more you find to enjoy and wonder about. If you were to linger over the "Little Betty Blue — Cobbler, Cobbler — Lucy Locket" page of Sylvia Long's *Mother Goose,* for example, you'd see Little Betty Blue minus one holiday shoe. On closer examination, however, you find it has tumbled onto the facing page into the path of Kitty Fisher, who has just found Lucy Locket's pocket. "Oh my goodness," you might imagine to yourself, "Kitty Fisher's going to find Betty's shoe, too, and hand it back to her across the page!"

And in case you wonder how Lucy Locket could have lost her pocket in the first place, you realize that Kitty Fisher has actually found a pocketbook, so *pocket* in this nursery rhyme is short for *pocketbook.* Further, you notice a pattern of green fish on Kitty Fisher's red dress. So Kitty Fisher, a cat, sports a fish-covered dress, which prompts you to look across the page at the cobbler dog's shirt pattern of — white dog bones! Whose shoes is the cobbler mending? You glance at Lucy Locket and Kitty

Fisher — no shoes on either one — but the red pair and the tan pair at the cobbler's match Lucy's and Kitty's dresses!

You might also notice the family of monarch butterflies and the escarpment on top of which Lucy is looking for her pocket in a small green bush. And this is just one set of facing pages out of 48! The anticipation of the detailed drawings on each page make this *Mother Goose* a pleasure to return to time and time again.

Words

Storybook word choice and usage influence children's speech and understanding. At the same time, children and adults generally understand text more complex than their own speech. Consider this example:

> *Opening [Beatrix Potter's* Peter Rabbit*] at random, you find "Peter gave himself up for lost, and shed big tears; but his sobs were overheard by some friendly sparrows, who flew to him in great excitement, and implored him to exert himself." There, in a nutshell, is a complete dramatic episode; the words are not taken from any approved list for pre-school children, but three- and four-year-olds have an instinctive perception of the meaning. And how they love to use them!* (Duff, p. 86).

Look for books in which writers, like Beatrix Potter, use words well. Children and adults alike take pleasure in pithy, imaginative "book" language, the music and humor of which often tumble, like Jack and Jill, into their own everyday speech. Watching a robin fly from a branch above the climber, four-year-old Jacob — echoing Mother Goose — said, "Look! We frightened Miss Robin away!"

Choose stories that are fun to read and hear because a particularly sonorous phrase appears and reappears at critical moments — for example, "Very well then, I will do it myself," from *The Little Red Hen* (Pinkney); "kuplink, kuplank, kuplunk!" from *Blueberries for Sal* (McCloskey); "Then I'll huff, and I'll puff, and I'll blow your house in," from *The Three Little Pigs* (Blegvad); and "A lovely light luscious delectable cake," from *The Duchess Bakes a Cake* (Kahl). Children and adults alike savor and often insert these phrases into their own conversations at the most surprising times!

Look for writers like William Steig who pack their stories with strong verbs and lots of action that make their stories particularly enjoyable to read with children, as you can hear in this excerpt from Steig's book *Farmer Palmer's Wagon Ride*:

> *In a while the road roughened and went through woods. As the wagon hobbled over the bumps, black clouds assembled and cast the earth in shadow. Harum-scarum gusts of wind turned the leaves this way and that. Then the rain they hoped for came, with scattered drops big as acorns slapping down, followed by a drubbing deluge.*

"World" or Place

In your storybook collection, include stories that take place in familiar settings children readily recognize and stories that magically transport you and the children out of your immediate surroundings. For example, you may go to Nashville, Tennessee (*Goin' Someplace Special,* McKissack), the Spanish countryside (*Ferdinand,* Lawson), a Lakota camp on the Great Plains (*Crazy Horse's Vision,* Nelson), a restaurant in Chinatown (*Apple Pie 4th of July,* Wong), Canada in the time of the voyagers (*A Dog Came, Too,* Manson), or Mali (*The Hatseller and the Monkeys,* Diakite). You might go to Sam-sam-sa-mara "where the animals and the people lived and worked together like they didn't know they weren't supposed to" (*Sam and the Tigers,* Lester) or the land of wooden blocks (*Changes, Changes,* Hutchins). Include books

Create a classroom book collection that offers children a variety of "worlds" to visit and return to again and again.

where you can live in the past, the present, or the future; a real place; or an imaginative world where animals talk and mingle with humans, fairies, giants, and "wild things." Psychologically, these places can be safe, reassuring, scary, strange, evocative, familiar, whimsical, puzzling, or absurd. The beauty is that children can enter and leave these worlds at will by opening or closing a book. They can venture forth on their own, with friends, or snuggled comfortably next to you or any other book-loving adult. In these places, they can encounter people who look like themselves and those who look and sound different but who often have needs, feelings, and experiences similar to their own.

Story Structure

Editors [of children's picture books] look for good, solid stories with beginnings, middles, and ends — a character and his dilemma; followed by the development, showing how that character manages to cope with his situation and change in some way to make it more acceptable; and a satisfying ending (Seuling, 2007, p. 38).

Narrative stories. Children, like editors, return again and again to books like the "funny monkey" story in which someone wants a problem solved. Such narrative stories form the core of a preschool book collection. The following discussion of the distinctive characteristics of narrative stories will give you an idea of what to look for.

Narrative stories include traditional tales like *The Three Billy Goat's Gruff* and *Little Red Ridinghood,* classic stories like *Caps for Sale* (Slobodkina) and *Blueberries for Sal* (McClosky), and newer stories like *Good Night, Gorilla* (Rathmann) and *Sam and the Tigers* (Lester). Regardless of publication date, they offer memorable *characters,* a familiar or engaging *setting,* and a *plot* that gives purpose to the characters' actions. In narrative stories, human or animal characters with recognizable dispositions and habits like curiosity, stubbornness, or the tendency to dawdle move the story along. The setting, such as a house, barn, park, forest, city, or village anchors the story in a particular reality. And the plot provides a coherent series of causally connected events or episodes that build on one another as characters face and work on problems that stand in the way of whatever they are trying to do.

Narrative stories present clearly stated *explicit information* in both the pictures and the text. For example, *Sven's Bridge* (Lobel) begins with a picture of Sven and the words "In a village by a river lived a man named Sven." In the picture on the next page, Sven stands next to the river across from his village on the other bank. As children return to look at, read, and talk about these stories with you and their peers, they begin to recognize and use these facts to figure out who the characters are, where the story takes place, what the problem is that drives the story along, what starts the problem, and how it gets resolved.

Narrative stories also rely on *implied information,* that is, meaning subtly offered or hinted at in the pictures and text but not directly stated. For example, a narrative story may suggest or give clues about what characters feel, what they plan or intend to do next, how events happen, why characters act the way they do, and what idea ties the whole story together. Gradually, with adult support, children begin to piece together the larger, implied meaning of a story beyond the literal facts. They figure out, for example, that the monkeys in *Caps for Sale* imitate the peddler and that in *Blueberries for Sal,* both Little Sal's mother and Little Bear's mother are startled to find themselves shepherding the other's child.

As children grapple with explicit and implied story information about characters, setting, and plot, they begin to hold story parts and elements in mind and understand the story as a coherent whole. Because narrative storybooks reveal new insights and provoke thought and conversation at each reading, they form the nucleus of a preschool book collection.

While the structural elements of narrative stories remains the same, format varies from book to book. For example, you will want to provide narrative stories like *Good Night, Gorilla* (Rathmann) and *Changes, Changes* (Hutchins) that rely completely on pictures or, like *Rosie's Walk* (Hutchins), *almost* completely on pictures to tell their tale. You will also want to include narrative stories like *Caps for Sale* (Slobodkina) and *David's Drawings* (Falwell) that combine pictures with a brief text as well as others like *Sam and the Tigers* (Lester) and *Farmer Palmer's Wagon Ride* (Steig) that include lengthier text along with detailed illustrations. Each format works, however, because children hunger for coherent stories about characters in predicaments. Will some of the words in the text puzzle them? Yes, of course, but over time and repeated readings, many of these words and phrases find their way into children's everyday conversation. As children's librarian, book seller, and parent Annis Duff says,

> *If children do not hear speech that has variety and liveliness, and if their books do not have unfamiliar words tucked in like bright surprises among the everyday ones, how in the world are they ever to accumulate a store of language to draw on, as new experiences and sensations increase the need and desire to communicate with the people they live with?* (p. 82)

Mother Goose. Your preschool storybook collection also needs the lilt and nonsense of Mother Goose nursery rhymes. These droll, and often dramatic, very short stories told in verse capture the sounds of the English language, add new words and lively expressions to children's everyday speech, and provide children with an abundance of rhyming word pairs to savor, say, and play with.

The Mother Goose nursery rhyme books currently in print vary mainly in format and illustration style. Photographs of children and adults in Brooklyn, New York, illustrate Nina Crew's *The Neighborhood Mother Goose.* Painter Sylvia Long populates her *Mother Goose* with animal characters and natural details. Animals and people with a slightly medieval flair scamper and dance through Tomie dePaola's *Mother Goose.* When you include all three volumes in your book collection, children begin to grasp the idea that a story, even a very short one, can be interpreted in more than one way. When they see Humpty Dumpty, for example, as an egg with a hand-drawn face in one book, as a rotund, bald gentleman in anther book, and as a yellow chick hatching from a broken eggshell in a third, they begin to understand that each artist "sees" the words his or her own way. And perhaps children will realize that they can create their own Humpty Dumpty images and other story character images as well.

Rhyming narrative stories. Finally, you will want to provide stories with characters, settings, and plots that are written completely in verse and accompanied by telling illustrations. In *The Duchess Bakes a Cake* (Kahl), for example, a Duchess who lives in a castle with the Duke and their 13 daughters decides that she's "going to make/ A lovely light luscious delectable cake." Once in the kitchen, she stirs up a batter. "She added the yeast, six times for good measure. / A light fluffy cake is really a pleasure." And therein lies the problem! The cake rises higher than the castle, with the Duchess on top of it. A lot of problem solving ensues until the youngest daughter's idea saves the day!

For examples of narrative storybooks for preschoolers, see "Narrative Stories" in the sidebar on pages 17–18.

So, to echo Beatrix Potter, let us exert ourselves to supply children with well-illustrated and well-written narrative storybooks and read them often, with pleasure, all the days of the preschool year — after we ourselves have spent time alone analyzing each book!

Story Analysis

Once you have selected a narrative storybook for your classroom, take time to become thoroughly familiar with it before reading it with children. When you spend time with a book on your own, you can see for yourself how the story is structured, look for new words in the text and illustrated in the pictures, and, most important, find what excites you about the book. You can then draw on this knowledge to sustain you through repeated readings of the story. The rest of this chapter provides a brief guide to story analysis that you can use as you familiarize yourself with books you plan to read with children.

Study the illustrations. What objects, animals, people, and actions do you see in the pictures? What objects and actions recur or reappear throughout the book? How did the artist make or render the pictures? With pen and ink? Oils? Fabric collage? Silk screen prints? Water colors? What design features, styles, or techniques does the artist use in each illustration? For example, do the pictures include borders, changing perspectives, stylized patterns, smooth lines, saturated colors, lots of white space, no white space, one scene per page, lots of separate pictures or events per page?

Jot down vocabulary words based on the pictures and text. Having a list at hand alerts you to words you can draw children's attention to gradually, a few words at a time, each time you read and talk about the story. You may want to organize the words you find and see illustrated into categories like names of objects and parts of objects (nouns); actions (verbs); ideas (nouns); and design features (nouns). Nouns that name items, animals, and people that children can point to in the pictures will be the easiest for them to grasp. At the same time, it is important to include action words — verbs like *jump, run,* and *sneak,* and idea words like *surprise, plan,* and *celebration.* The more children hear and use *any* word, the more they'll begin to make sense of its meaning and usage.

Figure out how the story is structured. Look for both the factual story elements that shape the narrative and the information suggested or implied by the pictures and words. As you figure out where the story takes place, who the characters are, what problem they face, and what they do to solve it, you will uncover the structural skeleton, or framework, of the story. Then, as you find and piece together implicit story clues, you'll begin to understand *how* the story works its magic. Ultimately, you'll appreciate the hard work preschoolers undertake as they assemble these facts and clues for themselves over repeated readings of the same story. The chart on page 16 outlines the course you might take in your analysis.

What Makes a Story Work?[1]

Story Elements to Identify

Somewhere (setting)
Someone (characters)
Wants (goal, initiating event)
A problem (conflict)
To be solved (solution, resolution/ending)

Implicit Story Information to Untangle

Feelings: Figure out what a character is feeling in a particular picture or situation.

Procedures: Figure out how an event or situation happens.

Causality: Figure out such things as the following:

- Why you think a character feels a particular way.
- Why a character is doing what he's doing.
- Why you think an event or situation happens.
- Why you think a particular event is an important part of the story.

Dialogue: Imagine what the characters in a picture might be saying.

Prediction: Anticipate the following:

- What you think a character will do next.
- What you think will happen next.
- What you think a character will do after the story is over.

Big Idea: Figure out the following:

- What big idea the story carries.
- What advice from the story you might consider if you were in a similar situation.
- What you might tell a friend if your friend were in a situation similar to the one in the story.

---

[1]This information is adapted from *Children's Comprehension of Narrative Picture Books* by Allison H. Paris and Scott G. Paris, listed in the references on page 59.

Storybooks for Preschoolers

The following storybooks include a variety of characters, settings, and plots. This sample list is not exhaustive but provides an idea of what to look for or where to start as you build a story collection.

Narrative Stories

Aardema, Verna. 1991/1998. *Borreguita and the Coyote.*

Ahlberg, Allen. 2006. *The Runaway Dinner.*

Armstrong, Jennifer. 2006. *Once Upon a Banana.* (wordless)

Arnold, Marsha D. 1995. *Heart of a Tiger.*

Bartlett, T. C. 1997. *Tuba Lessons.* (wordless)

Blades, Ann. 1999. *Wolf and the Seven Little Kids.*

Blegvad, Erik. 1980/1985. *The Three Little Pigs.*

Brett, Jan. 2002. *Daisy Comes Home.*

Bruchac, Joseph. 1998. *First Strawberries.*

Bruchac, Joseph. 2006. *Crazy Horse's Vision.*

Burningham, John. 1973/1983. *Mr. Gumpy's Motor Car.*

Burton, Virginia L. 1974. *Katy and the Big Snow.*

Burton, Virginia L. 1939/1977. *Mike Mulligan and His Steam Shovel.*

Choi, Yangsook. 2001. *The Name Jar.*

Day, Alexandra. 1985/1997. *Good Dog, Carl.* (wordless)

Demi. 1990/1996. *The Empty Pot.*

dePaola, Tomie. 1975/1979. *Strega Nona.*

dePaola, Tomie. 1978/1990. *Pancakes for Breakfast.* (wordless)

Diakite, Baba W. 1999/2000. *The Hatseller and the Monkeys.*

Egan, Tim. 2006. *Roasted Peanuts.*

Falwell, Cathryn. 2005. *David's Drawings.*

Freeman, Don. 2005. *Earl the Squirrel.*

Fox, Mem. 1989. *Night Noises.*

Gag, Wanda. 1928/2006. *Millions of Cats.*

Geeslin, Campbell. 2004. *Elena's Serenade.*

Gliori, Debi. 2001. *Flora's Blanket.*

Henkes, Kevin. 2000. *Wemberly Worried.*

Hoban, Russell. 1960/1995. *Bedtime for Frances.*

Hutchins, Pat. 1973/1987. *Changes, Changes.* (wordless)

Hutchins, Pat. 1968/1986. *Rosie's Walk.*

Kasza, Keiko. 1987/1996. *The Wolf's Chicken Stew.*

Keats, Ezra J. 1968/1998. *A Letter to Amy.*

Krauss, Ruth. 2005. *Bears.* (wordless)

Kroll, Steven. 1984/1993. *The Biggest Pumpkin Ever.*

Leaf, Munro. 1936/1964. *The Story of Ferdinand.*

Lehman, Barbara. 2007. *Rainstorm.* (wordless)

Lehman, Barbara. 2004. *The Red Book.* (wordless)

Lester, Julius. 2000. *Sam and the Tigers.*

Lindenbaum, Pia. 2001. *Bridget and the Gray Wolves.*

Lobel, Anita. 1965/1992. *Sven's Bridge.*

Lobel, Anita. 1979. *How the Rooster Saved the Day.*

Lowell, Susan. 1992. *The Three Little Javelinas.*

Manson, Ainslie. 2003. *A Dog Came, Too.*

McClintock, Barbara. 2006. *Adele & Simon.*

McClintock, Barbara. 1996/2004. *The Fantastic Drawings of Danielle.*

McCloskey, Robert. 1948/1976. *Blueberries for Sal.*

McCloskey, Robert. 1952/1976. *One Morning in Maine.*

McCloskey, Robert. 1941/1969. *Make Way for Ducklings.*

McDermott, Gerald. 1974/1977. *Arrow to the Sun.*

McKissack, Patricia C. 2001. *Goin' Someplace Special.*

Meyer, Mercer. 1967/2003. *A Boy, A Dog, and a Frog.* (wordless)

Montes, Marisa. 2000. *Juan Bobo Goes to Work.*

Mora, Pat. 2000. *Tomas and the Library Lady.*

Mosel, Arlene. 1977/1993. *The Funny Little Woman.*

Most, Bernard. 1990/2003. *The Cow Went Moo.*

Oppenheim, Shulamith L. 2003. *Hundredth Name.*

Parry, Florence H. 1995. *Day of Ahmed's Secret.*

Patrick, Denise Lewis. 1998. *Red Dancing Shoes.*

Pinkney, Jerry (illus.) 2006. *The Little Red Hen.*

Potter, Beatrix. 1902/2002. *The Tale of Peter Rabbit.*

Rathmann, Peggy. 1994. *Good Night, Gorilla.* (wordless)

Storybooks for Preschoolers (cont.)

Rey, H. A. 1941/1973. *Curious George.*
Rodanas, Kristina. 1995. *Dragonfly's Tale.*
Saki, Komako. 2003. *Emily's Balloon.*
Salley, Collen. 2002. *Epossumondas.*
Schaefer, Carole Lexa. 2004. *The Biggest Soap.*
Seeger, Pete. 1986/1994. *Abiyoyo.*
Sendak, Maurice. 1963/1988. *Where the Wild Things Are.*
Shannon, David. 2000/2002. *The Rain Came Down.*
Slobodkina, Esphyr. 1947/1987. *Caps for Sale.*
Soto, Gary. 1998. *Old Man and His Door.*
Smith, Cynthia Leitch. 2000. *Jingle Dancer.*
Spier, Peter. 1977/2002. *Noah's Ark.* (wordless)
Steig, William. 1974/1992. *Farmer Palmer's Wagon Ride.*
Steig, William. 1982/1990. *Doctor DeSoto.*
Steig, William. 1969/2005. *Sylvester and the Magic Pebble.*
Sweet, Melissa. 2005. *Carmine: A Little More Red.*
Tafuri, Nancy. 1984/1991. *Have You Seen My Duckling?*
Tekavec, Heather. 2002/2004. *Storm Is Coming!*
Tello, Jerry. 1997. *Abuela and the Three Bears.*
Turkle, Brinton. 1976/1992. *Deep in the Forest.* (wordless)
Varon, Sara. 2006. *Chicken and Cat.* (wordless)
Waddell, Martin. 1992/1996. *The Pig in the Pond.*
Waterton, Betty. 1996. *Salmon for Simon.*
Weittzman, Jacqueline P. 1998/2001. *You Can't Take a Balloon into the Metropolitan Museum.* (wordless)
Wiesner, David. 2006. *Flotsam.* (wordless)
Wiesner, David. 1991. *Tuesday.* (wordless)
Wiesner, David. 1988. *Free Fall.* (wordless)

Williams, Vera. 1982. *A Chair for My Mother.*
Winter, Jeanette. 2006. *Mamma.* (wordless)
Wong, Janet S. 2000. *The Trip Back Home.*
Wong, Janet S. 2002. *Apple Pie 4th of July.*
Zion, Gene. 1958/1976. *No Roses for Harry.*
Zion, Gene. 1956/1976. *Harry the Dirty Dog.*

Mother Goose

Crews, Nina. 2004. *The Neighborhoood Mother Goose.*
dePaola, Tomie. 1985. *Tomie dePaola's Mother Goose.*
Long, Sylvia. 1999. *Mother Goose.*
Opie, Iona. 1996. *My Very First Mother Goose.*

Rhyming Stories

Barracca, Debra and Sal. 1990/2000. *The Adventures of Taxi Dog.*
Bemelmans, Ludwig. 1967/2001. *Madeline.*
Bemelmans, Ludwig. 1953/2000. *Madeline's Rescue.*
Hoberman, Mary A. 1997/2000. *The Seven Silly Eaters.*
Kahl, Virginia. 1955/2002. *The Duchess Bakes a Cake.*
Komakiko, Leah. 1987/2003. *Annie Bananie.*
Newell, Peter. 2001. *The Slant Book.*

▼

Once you have selected books, enjoyed them, studied their illustrations, mined their vocabulary, and explored their structure and implicit meaning, you're ready to read them with children — often, with pleasure, and in ways that encourage children to look at, explore, and think about stories for themselves.

3
Conversation Basics: Invite Child Talk

"Converse during story reading? We didn't do that when I was a child!"

Child talk during story reading, once regarded as disruptive, is both a desirable and necessary form of story engagement. Rather than disrupting the flow of the story, focused child-adult talk during story reading actually helps children connect story parts and information into a meaningful whole. Figuring out stories presented in pictures and words happens inside the mind. So, to "get inside" children's minds to "see" how *they* understand stories, we encourage them to tell us what they think is going on.

Story comprehension — making sense of what characters do from one page or set of pictures to the next — unfolds gradually in children. To develop this skill, children rely on us to encourage them to identify what they see and hear and to connect this information to other characters and events in the story. Forming a coherent sense of story takes personal thought and talk over repeated readings and discussions of the same story. Simply listening to adults read and talk about stories is not enough for children to accomplish this task.

The skills children learn as they discuss and interpret the narrative sequences in illustrations serve them later as they read and interpret text. In fact, the process of making meaning from story illustrations is similar to the cognitive efforts children make to construct meaning from printed words (Paris & Paris, 2003).

The fewer people looking at one book, the more opportunities for story conversation.

Strategies for Inviting Child Talk

The following strategies promote children's story talk. You can use them each time you look at and read a story with children.

1. Read with individual and small groups of children. The fewer people looking at one book, the more opportunities for story conversation. This fact accounts, in part, for parents' unique ability to engage children in book reading. Seated on mom or dad's lap, a child has easy, direct contact with both reader and book and over time associates books and reading with a sense of pleasure and well-being.

In your own classroom, you will want to create a similar sense of intimacy and enjoyment as you read with children. With a child on your lap and a book in the child's hands, or with one or two children on either side of you and the book on the floor in front of you, you can make the book and yourself accessible and open for conversation.

2. Take a leisurely approach to story reading and book talk. Give children plenty of time to look at the pictures, think, and put their ideas into words. Young children need time to listen, look, consider, and transform what they understand into words. The more you engage in storybook reading and talk *at children's pace,* the more likely they are to contribute to story conversation.

3. Encourage children to engage physically with the book itself. As you read with children on your lap or close by your side, make sure they can see, touch, and point to the pictures, turn the pages, draw the book closer, and open and close the book as needed.

Some children may turn several pages at once. When this happens with no comment or corrective action from the child, examine and read the page the child turned to. Then, say something like "I think we skipped some pages. Let's turn back to look at them."

The more experience children have handling, looking at, and talking about books during story reading with you, the more opportunities they have to make sense of how books physically work.

In the lap of an adult, this child is able to open and close the book and see, touch, and point to the pictures.

4. Start with the pictures, then move to the text. Remember, preschoolers read pictures. They study them without regard to the text. So, instead of thwarting their strong desire to see and talk about the pictures, follow their lead and begin with the pictures. For example, you might say, "I wonder what you see on this page." After the children have looked and talked about what they see, you might say something like "Now let's see what the words tell us about the boy with the curly hair (or whatever)." While this practice may seem odd to you at first, you will find that children listen with more attention to the words once they have satisfied their desire to look at and talk about the pictures.

5. Have children do the lion's share of the talking. Whether you and the children are reading a wordless picture book together or are looking at the pictures in a word-full book, start with the children's descriptions of what they see in the pictures and build the story that emerges around their words and observations. The resulting story may seem a bit meager at first, but over time and with continued looking, thinking, and reading, the story the children see, hear, and tell will fill out as their understanding develops.

6. Listen to children — with interest. An attentive audience elicits child communication and talk. A child who senses your interest in his or her thoughts feels more confident about offering observations and ideas about the story than does a child who senses that you're mentally "out to lunch." While a child talks, follow what he or she says so you can grasp and incorporate the child's meaning into your response.

7. Elicit and respond to children's comments and observations. Story conversations proliferate when curious adults and children have the confidence to state their ideas out loud. If no one makes a spontaneous comment, invite children to tell you what they see by saying something like "I wonder what you see on this page." Use comments such as "The peddler looks different in this picture" to encourage conversation. Offer acknowledgments like "Hmm, he is missing his caps" and "Yes, I see" to keep it going.

When a child makes an observation such as "Mama duck," acknowledge the statement by saying something like "Yes, that does look like the mama duck."

8. Ask open-ended questions from time to time. What may seem apparent to you from a picture may convey an entirely different meaning to children, so go ahead and ask thought-provoking questions. For example, when looking at a puzzling picture, you might say, "What do you think the fox is doing in this picture?" or "How do you think the fox got covered with straw?" By asking the occasional question, you'll learn something about the children's story understanding.

9. Answer children's questions. When a child points to a pictured object and says, "What's that?" respond by answering the question. Depending on the child, you might say, "That's a cantaloupe," "That's a kind of fruit called a cantaloupe," or "The waitress is holding a cantaloupe, a large round fruit. It's a type of melon."

Spend as much time as children require on one page, looking at the pictures and responding to children's comments and questions. Even if children's questions seem

unrelated to the story, you may be pleasantly surprised at the connections children make for themselves and where their questions lead. Consider this exchange about *The Little Red Hen* (Pinkney):

Child: *(Points to the little red hen's leg)* What's that red on her leg? She hurt?

You: I see the red on her leg. And look, there's red on her other leg, too.

Child: And on this baby [chicken's] leg!

You: It looks like the red is a normal part of the skin on the chicken's legs.

Child: She got red leg skin!

You: Yes, the little red hen has red feathers and red leg skin!

10. Support children's ideas. Reading a story together with children, like any other human interaction, involves taking chances and problem solving. Since we want to encourage children's story talk, accepting children's story ideas and comments is more conducive to child talk than is negating or correcting them. Instead of telling children that they are wrong or are interpreting the story incorrectly, follow children's leads. Here, for example, is an exchange about an illustration in *The Little Red Hen* (Pinkney):

Child: It's up there! *(Points to a jar of jam on the shelf above the stove)*

You: There's the jar of jam on the shelf.

Child: She stood on here. *(Points to stove)*

You: Oh, so it looks like the hen might have stood on the stove to put the jam on the shelf.

Child: Uh oh! You can't stand there … on the stove!

You: Hmm.

Child: Maybe she jumped up …

11. Think aloud about the story from time to time. It makes sense to do this when you yourself have an idea about something in the story that hasn't occurred to you before. For example, your thinking out loud might spark a conversation that begins like this one:

You: *(Looking at a picture in* The Little Red Hen*)* You know what I just noticed? The ramp up to the little red hen's house is like the ramp on Rosie the hen's house!

Child: *(Leans closer to the picture)* These kinds of board things.

You: Yes, this ramp has the board things called slats, and Rosie's ramp has slats, too.

Child: I'll get *Rosie!* (*Get's the book* Rosie's Walk; *finds a hen house picture in that book; looks back and forth at the hen house pictures in the two storybooks*)

12. Create opportunities for children to think about the story. Rather than telling children everything you understand and want them to "get" about the story, you can help them develop the habit of figuring out stories for themselves — by offering comments and observations and asking the occasional thought-provoking question. As you do so, be patient with children's responses that may seem limited. Acknowledge their ideas and follow up with comments and prompts for elaboration. Children can articulate their own quite amazing ideas, but they need time, support, and practice. For example, an exchange involving children's thinking about *Rosie's Walk* might begin like this:

You: I wonder why the fox is in the pond.

Child: He jumped.

You: He did jump. What do you think made him do that?

Child: It ... so ... to get her. *(Points to Rosie)*

You: He jumped to get Rosie.

Child: He jumped in the pond to get Rosie.

You: He's in the pond and Rosie's still walking along ...

Try to probe for children's thinking without asking closed and fill-in-the-blank questions like "In this picture, Rosie is walking around the — what?" While such questions may be easier for children to answer, they do not engage children's thought or help them to do the mental work of understanding the story.

13. Flip back and forth in the story as needed. As you and the children look at, read, and talk and think about the story together, encourage the children to turn to related pictures; reread related text to the children as often as needed. This

While thinking and talking about a story together, encourage children to flip back and forth in the book to find related pictures.

practice helps children locate information they need to understand the story and connect characters, actions, and events from one part of the story to another. Although flipping back to an earlier page or ahead to a later one may seem disjointed, it actually helps children remember story parts and figure out how one story episode relates to another.

14. Read a book many times with children. This shouldn't be a problem since children typically want to read favorite stories over and over again. To maintain your enthusiasm, however, you can use a slightly different conversational focus each time, depending on where children are in their understanding of the story.

The strategies in the remainder of this book provide ideas about how to vary your readings and foster thought-provoking conversations from one storybook reading to the next.

4
Vocabulary: Learn New Words From a Story

One day on the playground, four-year-old Minnie calls to her teacher, "Hey, watch me!" As her teacher turns toward her, Minnie adds, "You be the watchman while I do this trick." Seconds later she revises her request: "I mean, you be the watchlady!"

A great deal of vocabulary acquisition occurs before children become literate (Biemiller, 2001). The storybook conversations you have with preschool children, for example, introduce them to object, action, and idea words used in story text and depicted in story illustrations. The teaching strategies in this chapter will help you converse about stories with vocabulary in mind and encourage children to consider and try out new words. But first, let's take a brief look at early vocabulary development.

Children learn new words by participating as active members of the local speech community. Enthusiastically attended to by parents, caregivers, and teachers, they are highly motivated to communicate their wants, needs, and interests.

In daily face-to-face interaction and communication with attentive, talkative adults, children hear, understand, and try out the power of word sounds, inflections, order, grammar, and meaning, as well as the social conventions of speech. Through these experiences, children build an ever-expanding bank of words they understand (receptive vocabulary) and words they use in their own speech (expressive vocabulary).

Children learn new words gradually as they hear and use them again and again. Learning the meaning of a word "is incremental — it takes place in many steps" (Nagy & Scott, 2000, p. 269). In other words, hearing a word once in a conversation or story is not enough. Hearing it defined once or using it once is not enough. Children must encounter and revisit words many times in many contexts, learning bit by bit what the words mean and how to use them. The more frequently children encounter a word, the more attuned they become to its multiple meanings and the shades of meaning that can shift with the context.

Equipped with a sizeable working vocabulary with which to articulate their thoughts, feelings, and ideas, children can navigate the process of learning to read with pleasure and confidence. The words they hear and begin to use in the preschool years are the words they will be able to understand when they encounter them in text later on as readers. The more words children have in their speaking vocabularies, the more likely they are to make sense of written text (Snow, Tabors, & Dickinson, 2001). Children who can sound out, recognize, and *understand* words are motivated readers. Children who do not understand the words they can sound out have little incentive to pursue such an unrewarding task.

For young children, vocabulary learning is a vital, dynamic process that advances step by step as you converse with them about stories and their daily lives.

Strategies for Learning New Words From Stories

The following strategies shift the focus of your storybook conversations with children to vocabulary building. You won't use them all every time you read with children, but you can draw on them at will as you reread favorite stories. The first two strategies you do on your own; the rest you use with children.

By Yourself

15. Look for unusual words in the text. You will find a few new-to-children words in some books and many new words in others.

Julius Lester, the author of *Sam and the Tigers,* for example, enjoys introducing several unusual words related to clothing: "The first place they went was Mr. Elephant's Elegant *Habiliments.* (Mr. Elephant liked words as big as him that nobody could say.)" Other stores Sam and his family visit include Monkey's Magnificent *Attire,* The Feline's Finest *Finery,* and Mr. Giraffe's Genuine Stupendous Footwear *Emporium.*

In *Farmer Palmer's Wagon Ride,* William Steig uses unusual words abundantly with an emphasis on **nouns** *(barnacles, burden, chest, deluge, encouragement, frenzy, harmonica, harness, hock, homeward, lantern, noggin, opinion, poultice, predicament, quarts, sarsaparilla, shafts, sunrise, sunstroke, traces, tripod, wainwrights)* and

After looking at a book on your own, draw on the words you noted in text and pictures when reading with children.

verbs *(buckling, bulged, clattering, descending, exhausted, extracting, gawking, hobbled, jolted, lugged, mumbling, opined, propelled, quench, quivered, roughened, somersaulted, straddled, swerving, tip-hoofed, winced).*

16. Attune yourself to the words offered by the pictures. Just as you "mine" the text of a story for new words, you can think of words that describe the objects and actions depicted in the book's illustrations. Each illustration offers an astonishing potential picture vocabulary. You can open any storybook and list the nouns and verbs waiting there for you to see and talk about in each picture! For example, a *beginning* list of words hiding in plain sight in Peggy Rathmann's illustrations for *Good Night, Gorilla* might look like this:

> **Animals names and parts (nouns):** *armadillo, brush, elephant, giraffe, gorilla, hoof, horns, hyena, lion, mane, mouse, paw, shell, spots, tail, toes, tongue, trunk, tuft, tusk, vulture*

> **Clothing-and-people-related names (nouns):** *belt loop, belt, brim, buckle, cap, hat, husband, mustache, nametag, nightcap, nightgown, partner, patch, pocket, shirt, slippers, tie, uniform, visor, wife, zookeeper*

> **Gorilla actions (verbs):** *balance, carry, climb, copy, cover, crawl, creep, cross, drag, enter, eye, feel, fit, follow, grab, grin, hang, hide, hold, hush, imitate, lead, lean, leave, lie, look, lower, march, open, play, point, quiet, reach, scoot, sit, sleep, smile*

With Children

17. Invite children to talk about what they see in pictures. Pause on each two-page spread and say something like "I wonder what you see on this page." Give children plenty of time to look at the pictures and talk about the objects, animals, people, and actions they see. Listen for the words *they* use to describe what they see and incorporate their words and phrases into your comments and observations.

18. Incorporate some of the book's vocabulary into your own comments and observations. Draw on the words you noted as you looked at the pictures and read the text on your own. For example, looking at the picture of the mouse with his banana in front of the lion's cage in *Good Night, Gorilla,* you might have the opportunity to use the word *drag* in an exchange like this:

Child:　He still got the banana!

You:　Mouse still has the banana. He's dragging it along behind him.

Child:　On a string!

This teacher listens for the words the children use to talk about what they see in the storybook pages.

You: The banana is tied on a string so mouse can hold the string and drag the banana along!

Child: *(Flips back to an earlier picture, points to the mouse)* Holding banana. *(Flips back to the current page)* Do this … drag.

You: Yes, in that picture the mouse holds the banana. In this picture he drags the banana!

19. Use synonyms, definitions, and root words. Multiple words for the same object, action, or idea help children begin to make sense of new words and expand their store of words. When children encounter unfamiliar words in the pictures and text, you can provide synonyms, that is, words with similar meaning, like *pig* and *hog*; definitions; explanations of word meanings, such as a ship is a very big boat; and root words — words that have the same root or origin, such as *laugh* and *laughter*.

Using words and their synonyms, definitions, or root words in the same conversation links words that are new for children to known words and familiar contexts. Here is an example of a story-talk exchange about the meaning of the word *shrug*.

You: *(Reading from* Sam and the Tigers*)* "Sam looked at Sam. Sam shrugged. Sam shrugged back. Sam … "

Child: What's shrugged? It's funny.

You: *Shrugged* is a funny sounding word. I wonder if you've ever seen anyone shrug their shoulders.

Child: You mean like this? *(Shrugs)*

You: Yes, exactly! You're raising your shoulders, bending your arms, and holding your palms up. You're shrugging!

Child: Huh! Like in the picture. *(Pointing to Sam's dad)*

You: Yes, like Sam's dad. He's shrugging. I wonder what you think he might be saying as he shrugs.

Child: *(Shrugs)* I don't know.

You: Exactly — you shrug when you don't quite know. Shrugging is a way of saying "I don't know" or "Maybe."

20. Look up words in the dictionary with children. Keep an adult dictionary close at hand. When you come across a word you don't know, can't remember, or wonder how to pronounce, like the word *habiliments* in *Sam and the Tigers,* turn to the dictionary. Your conversation about habiliment might begin something like this:

You: *(Reading)* "The first place they went was Mr. Elephant's Elegant Habiliments." Hmm. I'm not sure how to say *habiliments* or what it means.

Child: *(Looking at the picture of Mr. Elephant holding a jacket)* Maybe jackets.

You: Maybe it does mean jackets. That's an idea! Let's look in the dictionary. *(You find the word* habiliment *in the dictionary.)* It says *habiliments* means clothes — jackets, shirts, pants.

Child: 'Biliments is jackets, and clothes and all this other stuff he's selling!

Although you may associate dictionaries with older children who read and write papers, preschoolers make great dictionary lovers. No one expects them to use a dictionary with speed and correctness. Young children who grow up with dictionaries, using them with adults in unpressured situations, develop "the dictionary habit" — so don't hesitate to put your dictionary to use as needed during story reading.

21. Connect words to children's gestures and emerging ideas. Focus on nouns and verbs — objects and actions. As you look with a child at *Good Night, Gorilla,* for example, the child may point to the armadillo on the floor in the zookeeper's room. In response, you might say something like "There's the armadillo. Armadillo is curled up next to the hyena at the foot of the zookeeper's bed." Or a child might point to the yawning gorilla and say "Tired," to which you might respond by filling out the idea:

As you look at books with children, point out illustrations of nouns and verbs and connect them to children's gestures and emerging ideas.

"Yes, gorilla does look tired. He's yawning!"

22. Encourage children to try out action words they see in pictures and hear in text. Children add new words to their vocabulary through action and experience, so acting out words helps children understand what the words mean. As you talk together about how a character moves, for example, pause from time to time for children to do the same motions and through their own actions begin to make sense of words like *sneak, dance, hop, dart,* and *flop.*

23. Draw children's attention to the vocabulary of design. As picture readers, children spend lots of time studying and finding meaning in storybook illustrations. So, from time to time, you have the opportunity to shift your focus from what the pictures mean to how they work as illustrations. That is, you support children's visual literacy. To spark a conversation about familiar illustrations, you might make comments like the following about colors, lines, and page design:

> "It looks like the artist drew this picture using only black and white."
>
> "I wonder what you notice about the colors on this page."
>
> "I don't think I've ever seen so many shades of blue (green, purple, or whatever)."
>
> "It looks like the artist used lots of straight (curved, jagged, zigzag, smooth, twisty, rippling, short, hatched, looping, spiral, diagonal, or whatever) lines to make this picture."
>
> "There seem to be a lot of small pictures on this page. I wonder why."
>
> "I see a border around this picture. It's made of colored lines (one green line, feathers, ribbons, flowers, vines, bamboo, dots, mesh, a honeycomb pattern, or whatever)."

24. Encourage children to look for and talk about recurring design features. Once children have noticed how the illustrator uses color, lines, and designs on a page, encourage them to see what similar features appear on other pages throughout the story. For example, you might say something like the following:

"I think I've seen scalloped edges like these before."

"I wonder if all the pages have black and white pictures (scalloped edges, birds in the corners, swirls of color, footprints at the bottom, or whatever)."

Listen to and support children's observations as they note a particular design element and flip back and forth to find where it reappears. As a result of using this strategy, children often begin to incorporate similar design features into their own drawings and paintings.

25. Use words and phrases from stories in your everyday conversations with children. Later on in the day when you're engaged with children in other non-story conversation and play, insert storybook words and phrases into your comments and observations both for enjoyment and connecting storybook words to a real-life context. For example, you might make comments like these:

"Look — gusts of wind are blowing the leaves off the trees!"

"We're playing inside today because it's raining so hard. It's a drubbing deluge with raindrops slapping down!"

"Please, I implore you to think about what you plan to do at work time!"

"I see some of our dress-up finery still lying on the floor!"

"Today for lunch we're having some lovely light luscious delectable lettuce!"

Listen for and support children's use of storybook words in their own conversation. And remember to use new words regularly; children need to hear and use a word many times to make it "their own."

5
Connection: At Home in a Story

"Look," says Joseph in a flash of recognition while looking at one of his favorite books, Blueberries for Sal *(McCloskey). "Little Sal and her mom have pails!" (He flips ahead to a picture of Little Bear and his mom.) "And they have no pails. Just their mouths!"*

To understand a story narrative, children relate the story to something that already makes sense to them. In other words, they *make connections.* When a child looking at *Rosie's Walk* (Hutchins) says, "Rosie the hen takes a walk. Hey, I take walks with my Nana," the child builds a mental bridge that connects his or her actual experience of taking a walk with the made-up world of the story in which a hen takes a walk.

To make sense of the story, young children also work to connect the story parts to the whole story (Paris, 2004). That is, they figure out what is going on during each story event or episode (for example, when the fox jumps and lands on the rake), hold each episode in mind, and connect a series of remembered episodes into a coherent story — in this case, a story about the relationship between Rosie and the fox as Rosie takes a walk before dinner and the fox tries to catch her for his dinner. While the connection between one event and the next in *Rosie's Walk* is readily apparent to us adult readers, it is not to a young child. Preschool children must construct these connections for themselves with the patient support of teachers and parents. Otherwise, they see the story as a series of snapshots or postcards in which each page or two-page spread is a story complete in itself.

Strategies for Making Connections

The strategies in this chapter shift the focus of storybook reading and conversations to helping children make connections to and across the story, both to hook it to their own lives and knit one part of the story to the next. Although you would not use all of these strategies during a single storybook reading, it might be particularly beneficial to draw on them as you read and talk about a story the first several times and from time to time thereafter.

26. Encourage children to talk about objects, animals, and people they see in illustrations on the cover and pages of the book. The first things children typically see and name in storybook pictures are objects, people, and animals, just as names — such as *milk, mama, dog,* and *kitty* — are the first words they generally say when learning to talk. As children picture-read, naming characters and objects they see, they form an idea about the story subject and often refer to a book in shorthand form based on this understanding, as in the following examples:

"Let's read the funny monkey book!"

"I'll get the chicken book."

"Where's the shoe book?"

Invite children to look and then talk about what they see by saying something like "I wonder what you see on the cover" or "Hmm — there are lots of things to see on this page." Pause for children to gather their ideas. Listen to and acknowledge their contributions. If no one makes an observation, you might point out and name an object yourself; for example, "I see a little girl" or "I see chickens." Repeat this process for each picture.

When adults encourage children to talk about what they see on the cover and pages of a book, they help children form an idea about the story subject.

27. Converse with children about things in pictures they have seen or played with themselves. To encourage such a conversation, you might begin with a comment like "I wonder what you see in this picture that's like something you play with (you have in your house, you've seen on a walk, we have in our classroom, or whatever)."

If, after children have had time to look and consider, no one offers a response, you might say something like "Hmm, the inside of the goat family's house looks like the inside of a person's house." Or you might say, "There are lots of baskets in this picture. Some are like the baskets we use in our classroom."

Listen to and support children's responses and tie their experiences to the story. For example, you might have an exchange like this one about a picture in *Sam and the Tigers* (Lester):

You:	I wonder if you have any clothes like the ones Sam's wearing in this picture.
Child:	I got purple, a purple skirt.... And a 'brella.
You:	You have a purple skirt like Sam's purple pants, and you have an umbrella, too.
Child:	My mom has a big one with that part. *(Points to umbrella handle)*
You:	Your mom has a big umbrella with a curved handle like Sam's.
Child:	Yep.
You:	So Sam is outside in his purple pants like your purple skirt, his big umbrella with the handle like your mom's umbrella, and his other new clothes.

28. Encourage children to make connections between what they see in the pictures and hear about in the text. You can use this strategy after you've looked at and talked about the pictures in the story. For example, you might say something like "Now that we've looked at all the pictures to get an idea of who this story is about, let's find out what the words tell us about the girl and her chickens (or whomever)."

A book's illustrations help children make connections and feel at home in a story.

Another time, rather than looking at all the pictures in the book and then reading the words, you might look at the picture on one page or on a two-page spread and then read the words on that page or two. For example, you might look at and talk about the picture on the first page of *Daisy Comes Home* (Brett) and then say, "Let's hear what the words say about the chickens and the water (or whatever the children have noted)."

There may be times when you go the other way, that is, connect the text to the pictures. For example, after reading in *Daisy Comes Home* the line "A dog was sitting on the deck of the houseboat," you might pause and say something like "I wonder where the deck of the houseboat is in the picture."

When reading a wordless picture book, like *Pancakes for Breakfast* (dePaola), for example, you might say something like "This story has no words, just pictures. Let's see what the pictures tell us about the lady and her pancakes." Eventually, as children gain experience looking at and talking about pictures, and as they begin to soak up some of the more formal speech of story text, you might say something like "Let's tell the story of *Pancakes for Breakfast* as if we were the person writing the words for it." Gradually, you might hear children using "book language," including narrative phrases like "Once upon a time," "'Oh, dear,' said the lady," "The lady in the purple dress thought about pancakes all the way home," and so forth.

29. Encourage children to comment on *actions* they see and hear about in the story. For example, as you look at a book with children, you can attempt to focus the conversation on actions by saying something like the following:

"I wonder what you see happening on this page."

"Hmm. What do you see the fox doing in this picture?"

"Let's see what Sam is doing on this page."

"I wonder what you see gorilla doing now."

Given the two-dimensional nature of illustrations, we tend to see characters and objects more readily than actions since action in a still picture can only be caught midstream. At the same time, characters' actions drive the story along. And knowing and using action words enables children to move

The book this child selects will likely have a cover illustration she connects with from a previous look at the book or another experience.

from single-word utterances like "Horsey!" to complete thoughts or sentences like "Horsey runs!"

Focusing on actions in the story equips children with the language to combine an object with an action to form a complete thought or sentence and thus begin to comprehend the movement or flow of the story from one situation to the next.

30. Encourage children to relate actions in stories to their own actions. To do this, you might try comments like these:

> "The mouse is dragging the banana on a string. I'm wondering how you move something that's about the same size as you."

> "Gorilla stands on his tiptoes to reach the lock on the lion's cage. I wonder what you do when you can't reach something."

> "I wonder if you see Frances the raccoon (or whoever the character is) doing things that you sometimes do at bedtime."

Although many children's books feature animal characters, their actions speak directly to children because the characters find themselves in situations that children themselves face — getting ready for bed, losing something, taking a walk, not doing what their mom has told them to do, helping with chores, getting into mischief, getting lost, getting dirty, and so forth.

As children grow and accumulate experiences, they organize what they know into schemata, or related sequences, for easy access later on (Anderson & Pearson, 1984). Therefore, when a child hears about or sees a picture of Frances the raccoon waking up her father in the middle of the night to tell him "There is a monster under my bed!" a child with similar bedtime fears and experiences identifies with the character and enters into the story with an experience-based sense of ease and anticipation. Even though the character may be an animal, or may be in a bedroom that looks different from the child's, the child follows along with interest because he or she, too, has difficulty going to bed and is scared at night.

After reading a story and concentrating on the actions in it, you might say, "So, the characters in *Bedtime for Frances* (or whatever book you're reading) do things like things we do."

31. Identify recurring characters, objects, and actions with children. When in previous story readings children have named and talked about characters and actions in a story, you might shift the focus a bit by saying something like the following:

> "Here's gorilla again!"

> "There's a balloon on this page, too!"

> "I wonder if we will see Sam (the mouse, the keys, Rosie walking, the chicken floating in the basket) again in another picture."

> "I wonder if we'll hear more about the man and his door."

Finding things, people, and actions that reappear throughout a story helps children connect one story part to the next and form an idea of the story as an unfolding sequence of related events. In a sense, the recurring item serves as a continuous thread that weaves its way from one end of the story to the other.

32. Encourage children to figure out *where* an action or scene is happening. To draw children's attention to the setting of the story, say something like the following:

Finding objects, people, and actions that recur throughout a story helps children connect story parts and form an overall idea of the narrative.

> "I wonder where this story is happening."

> "I wonder what kind of place the picture on the cover shows."

> "I see a (tree, chair, bus, or whatever) that might give us a clue about the place we see."

> "I wonder what you know from your own experience about (this kind of place)."

Noticing where the action takes place in a story orients the child. It may also prompt the child to connect his or her own kitchen or clothing store experiences, for example, to the kitchen or clothing store in the story.

33. Draw children's attention to critical parts or episodes of the story. You can do this by making comments like these:

> "Let's see what happens in this part of the story."

> "It looks like something different is happening. I wonder what you see now."

> "It looks like something different is happening in this part of the story."

> "It looks like this part of the story changes to (happens in) a different place."

As the children look at the pictures that show a critical part of the story, say something like the following:

"I wonder what's going on in this part of the story."

"What do you think is happening now?"

Noticing and talking about story parts helps children begin to understand that stories have beginnings, middles, and ends; that what happens in one part of the story is causally related to what happens in the next; and that stories unfold in coherent, rather than random, sequences of events.

34. Look at and read the story episode by episode. Another day, when the child or children you are reading with have some idea about the episodes in a particular story, you might say something like "Let's read and talk about the first part of the story." Then, have the children put a bookmark wherever in the story *they* think the first part of the story ends.

After looking at, reading, and talking about that episode, say something like "Let's read and talk about the next part of the story when the peddler wakes up from his nap (Sam goes off to school, the goats are in the house by themselves, or whatever)." Invite the children to put a marker at the end of that episode. Continue episode marking, reading, and talking in this manner through the rest of the story.

35. Look for and talk about *emotions* depicted in pictures and text. For example, you might invite children to look for story clues about emotions by making comments like the following:

"I wonder what feelings you think Sam (the family, the girl, or whoever) on the cover is showing."

"I wonder what you think Sam (or whoever) is feeling right now in this picture."

"As we read the story, let's listen for and talk about clues the words give us about Sam's (or whoever's) feelings."

You might also find occasion to make follow-up comments like "I wonder how you feel when, like the peddler, you lose something important to you."

36. Encourage children to talk about *ideas* they see and hear about in a story. More abstract and less immediately visible than characters, objects, actions, and perhaps even feelings, the ideas in children's stories — surprise, celebration, stalling at bedtime, dressing up, trickery, planning, searching — typically represent basic aspects of human nature. For children who might be curious and interested in the "big idea" behind a story, you might make comments like these:

"I love reading this book (fill in the title) with you! I wonder what you think the cover shows about the idea of (stepping out in fine clothes, playing and spying, or whatever idea is behind the story)."

"Let's see what the pictures tell us about the idea of … "

"Let's see what clues the words give us about the idea of … "

37. Encourage children to invent words or dialogue for characters in a particular illustration or situation. This helps children imagine what a character might be thinking and discover implied information children need to make sense of the story. For example, you might say something like "What do you think the mouse (or whoever) might be saying in this picture?" or "I wonder what the little girl is thinking now."

38. Ask children to tell *why* they think something happens in the story. With children who have read and talked about a book enough times to have a sense of the story as a whole, take time when the occasion arises to encourage their thinking about why things happen in the story as they do. For example, you might say something like "That's funny. Sam tells the tiger that his shoes are ear-shoes! I wonder why he says that." Or "It says, 'Seems like five Tigers had disappeared that morning and nobody could find them. Sam smiled but didn't say a word.' I wonder why Sam didn't say anything about the tigers." As always, listen to and acknowledge children's ideas and continue to probe their thinking as needed.

39. Support children's new ideas, connections, and changing understanding of the story over time. One of the satisfactions of reading the same books over and over again with children is watching their understanding of the story change and grow. For example, looking at the page in *Good Night, Gorilla* in which the zookeeper says good night to the armadillo, a three-year-old says, "dillo" and "bottle" as he points to the armadillo and the baby bottle in her pen. As a four-year-old, after many return visits to this book, the same child looks at the same page and says, "Where's her armadillo toy? Lion has a lion toy, and gorilla has a gorilla toy. Where's hers?" By age five, this child brings his own experience as a big brother to the story and says with confidence, "Armadillo *does* have a toy armadillo. But, you can't see it in the picture. She hid it from her baby sister!" It's our job to appreciate and support the child's observations and thinking at each step along the path of story comprehension.

40. Play "I Spy." Depending on the child you are reading with, occasionally take time to spy, and then have the child find, an object, character, action, event, or idea you've talked about in a previous read-together session. For example, you might say, "On this page, I spy the keys to the animals' cages, but they are not with the zookeeper!" And then turn the spying role over to the child. This strategy, like the others in this chapter, helps children grasp the essential narrative elements that come together to make the story work as a coherent whole.

6
Retelling: Remember a Story

"You know what?" says Angelo, lying on his cot at rest time, clutching a small dump truck. He addresses his teacher, referring to his current favorite book, Mike Mulligan and His Steam Shovel *(Burton). "I think Mike really, really likes Mary Anne the steam shovel, so that's why he always stays with her. She digs very, very fast, even faster than anything!"*

Retelling stories and parts of stories personally engages children in the complex thinking required to actively construct meaning, understand narrative stories, and participate in the story-forming process (Paris & Paris, 2003). By mentally forming and then articulating their own narratives based on what they have seen, heard, understood, and interpreted, children actively construct memory (Bolles, 1988). Retelling helps children create the narrative structure that will enable them to refer to, use, and elaborate on the story's main narrative elements again and again for the rest of the their lives (Shank, 1990). When children retell some or all of the story, they are saying, in effect, "There! I've got it! It's mine!" Once children recall book items and events, they do not quickly forget them (Cornell, Senechal, & Bodo, 1988).

Retelling also allows children to enter into the lives of the story characters, to speak on their behalf, and to connect their own experiences to the characters' — and in doing so, to comprehend what the characters are doing and saying. Figuring out why things happen is especially important in increasing children's vocabulary

Story retelling helps children make connections between pictures, pictures and text, parts of the story, and their own experiences.

and comprehension (Clarke-Steward & Beck, 1999). Retelling helps preschool children develop critical narrative skills without which they are likely to have difficulty in school in general and with literacy in particular (Feagans, 1984; Roth, 1986).

Through recalling or retelling information from a story, children put their thoughts into words, trying out new words and ideas. At first, children tend to make brief statements about something that just happened in the story or about a recurring character, animal, or object. With experience and support, they retell and/or reenact a favorite part or parts of the story, often including one or two details. Gradually, children progress to retelling parts or all of the story in some detail. They often include language from the text in retelling, can retell or organize events from the story in sequence, and may say *why* things happen in the story.

Strategies for Retelling

The strategies in this chapter can help you focus some of your story readings and conversations on recalling and remembering story characters and events. You can draw on them from time to time as you revisit stories, and you may find them particularly effective after children have made some connections to and across the story you are reading and talking about together.

During Story Reading

41. Refer to the book's cover illustration from time to time. Often, the first thing a child remembers about a book is the cover, so it makes sense to make use of it as a reference for retelling. For example, while looking at a picture on the title page, you might have the occasion to say something like the following:

"I think we've seen this picture before."

"These goats (or whatever) look like the ones we saw on the cover."

Enjoy and support the conversation that follows as children flip back and forth to compare the two illustrations.

At another reading, you might read aloud the title of the story and then say something like the following:

"Oh, I think I have heard those words before."

"It looks like the name of the book is on this title page and on the cover!"

Again, support children who flip back and forth to check. You can also use this strategy when you come across an illustration in the body of the book that calls to mind the cover illustration. For example, you might make comments like these:

"Now all the goats are outside again, like they were on the cover of the book."

"Gorilla has his finger to his lips in this picture just like he did on the cover!"

"Daisy's in the basket again just like she was on the cover, but this time the basket's floating down the river!"

Again, pause for some flipping back and forth as children make their own observations.

At a later reading when children are familiar with the book, you might begin by saying something like the following:

"When you look at the cover, I wonder what you remember about *who* this story is about."

"I wonder what the cover helps you remember about *what* happens in this story."

"I wonder what the cover reminds you about *where* this story takes place."

42. As you look at, read, and talk about a story, pause from time to time for children to recall where in the story they have seen or heard about the same characters, objects, or actions. For example, to encourage such recollections, you might say something like the following:

"Here's the man with the green shirt again!"

"I think maybe we've seen this little girl (basket, house, balloon, or whatever) before on an earlier page."

"It looks like Daisy's still floating down the river in her basket!"

"It seems like we've heard another tiger say these very same words to Sam!"

This teacher encourages these children's retelling by occasionally pausing for the children to recall characters, objects, or actions from an earlier point in the story.

"I wonder if you see anything in this picture that you've seen before in an earlier picture."

Listen to and support children's recollections and their need to flip back through the book to verify them.

43. Pause from time to time to encourage children to recall an earlier part of the story. This strategy helps children begin to relate past story actions and events to the ones they are currently seeing and hearing about. Here are examples of the kinds of things you might say to provide opportunities for such recollections:

> "Wait a minute! The peddler has just one cap on his head (Sam is wearing his underwear, all the animals are in the house, or whatever). It wasn't like that earlier in the story!"

> "Before we read any more, I wonder what you remember about (the story so far; the fox; what happened in the zoo)."

> "I wonder what you remember about Mei Mei before she takes her eggs to the market."

> "So Daisy had some adventures on the river. I wonder what you remember about them."

As always, listen to and support children's recollections and their desire to flip back to earlier pages to help them along.

At the End of the Story

44. Encourage children to find an illustration they particularly like and retell that part of the story. For example, you might say something like "I wonder if you can go back to your favorite page in this story and talk to me about it." Since most children find some story event or illustration particularly appealing, they are willing to turn to that page — where all the tigers chase each other, the little goat hides in the clock, all the lights go out, or whatever — and relive it with gusto! This strategy eases children into story retelling in a way that's accessible to even the youngest child.

At later readings of the same story, you might encourage children to select, turn to, and retell two of their favorite story parts or pages. Eventually, some children might enjoy the challenge of selecting a page from the beginning of the story, a page from the middle of the story, and a page from the end of the story to retell. As you use this strategy over time, you will probably notice that gradually children's retellings expand as they begin to retell parts of the story that occur before and after the pictures they've selected.

45. Consider using storyboards to encourage retelling. One way to help children see stories as a whole and retell them is to take a storybook apart, lay out the pages in lines or rows and, in effect, create a continuous story panorama or scroll. You can do this by making storyboards (for instructions, see the sidebar on the opposite page, "Storyboards"). Although you won't do this with every story you read with children, it's worth making storyboards for at least one or two stories because of what both you and the children will learn from seeing a story in this format.

With both the storybook and the storyboards in hand, say something like "We've been reading *Blueberries for Sal* together. Here's a different way to look at and read the same story." Together with the child, arrange the storyboards in order in a line,

Storyboards

What They Are

Storyboards are the two-page spreads that result from taking apart and reassembling the pages of a children's storybook.

Storyboards make it possible for children to see an entire story spread out before them at once. This experience is different from seeing the story unfold one two-page spread at a time, as it does in book form.

Where They Come From

Actually, picture books start out as storyboards. To make a picture book, the illustrator creates a series of paintings or drawings that are displayed simultaneously for examination and reference. Later, when the illustrations and text are integrated and printed, the resulting pages are bound in book form for efficiency and easy handling. As a book, the illustrations now appear one two-page spread at a time.

In a way, unbinding a storybook to create a series of storyboards returns the illustrations and text to their original, prepublication form.

How They Help

Laying out a story as a series of storyboards helps children build a sense of story. It helps them see and understand stories as coherent wholes in which characters engage in connected actions and events to solve a particular problem or carry out a purpose.

How to Make Them

You will need
- A copy of the storybook you are reading
- Two additional paperback copies of the same storybook
- Construction paper
- Tape (matte finish or "magic" tape, not transparent cellophane or masking tape)
- Clear contact paper (or laminating tools).

1. Carefully take apart the **two** paperback storybooks.

2. Using the pages from both books, tape together each two-page spread of the story into a storyboard.

3. Spread all the storyboards story face up in lines or rows so you can see the whole story from start to finish.

4. Check the storyboards against the original, intact copy of the book to make sure you have storyboards for the entire story.

5. Cover the backs of the storyboards with construction paper (since these pictures and text will be out of order and confusing if visible).

6. Number the back of each storyboard in order.

7. Cover each storyboard with clear contact paper or laminate (optional).

in rows, or in a circle, for example, referring to the bound book to check the order as needed. As you do this task, listen to and support the child's observations about this process and whatever he or she notices about seeing the story in this fashion. This conversation in itself may be enough for one session.

When you use the storyboards again from time to time, comments like the following can encourage retelling:

"When you look at this whole story, I wonder what part is your favorite."

A child's reenactment of part of a story helps him develop his ideas about what happens in the overall story and connect one part to another.

"It looks like fox (Sam, the goats, or whoever) has some problems in this story. I wonder which problems you can remember when you look at these storyboards."

"We usually tell the story of gorilla (Little Sal, or whomever) when we look at this book. Maybe you could look at these storyboards and tell the story of another character like the mouse (Little Bear, or whomever)."

46. From time to time, encourage children to recall and draw, model, or reenact something they liked from the story. Representing story characters and events on paper, with clay, or through physical action and imitation is another way for young children to recall and retell story parts and events.

You can anticipate that young children's drawings, models, and reenactments will generally begin as very simple ones with few details — a face with arms and legs emerging from it for the zookeeper, a blob of clay for gorilla, a smaller blob for mouse, pretend sleeping to represent the animals asleep at the zookeeper's house. Over time and with experience, children's representations of stories in any medium will grow in detail and complexity. In the meantime, no matter how they choose to draw, model, or reenact gorilla with his keys, Little Sal or Little Bear, or Sam meeting a tiger, the words they use to explain what they have made or done will help them consolidate their understanding of this particular character or event.

Whenever you encourage a child to use one of these media, support his or her choices, depictions, and explanations. For these representations to arise from the child makes more sense to the child than, for example, if you were to provide props and instructions for reenacting the entire story. Although children's ideas may sometimes seem extraordinarily simple to you, the children find them very satisfying because their ideas make sense to them. A child's reenactment of *Caps for Sale,* for example, might include walking while pretending to balance a "head full" of caps on his or her head, or pretending to fall asleep under a tree, or stamping feet and yelling, or pretending to be a monkey in a tree, all depending on which part of the story strikes the child's fancy. Eventually, the child may add another action or part of the story to his or her reenactment.

47. Wonder out loud about *changes* that occur in the story, and listen to children's ideas. Considering change is one way to organize story thoughts and understanding. So, occasionally after looking at, reading, and talking about a story, encourage a child to recall what changes in it. For example, you might say something like the following:

> "It seems as if things changed in this story. Let's see if we can remember one thing that changed."
>
> "I wonder how you think Sam (the tigers, Sam's dad or whoever) changed in this story."
>
> "I wonder what changed for Daisy the hen (Mei Mei, the fisherman, or whomever) in this story."

A child may or may not flip back through the story looking at pictures for clues.

Thinking about change in a story challenges children and adults alike; so, as ever, support children's efforts no matter how they diverge from your own. Once children develop and enjoy the habit of thinking about how stories work and what they mean to them, their capacity for story comprehension knows no bounds.

48. Wonder out loud *why* story events unfold as they do and listen to children's ideas. Occasionally, at the end of a story, encourage children to think back about why something happens or why a character acts in a particular way. Again, this strategy helps organize children's recall and story retelling in a slightly different manner and helps children look back in the story for clues about cause and effect. To initiate such conversations, you might say something like the following:

> "I wonder why you think gorilla let all the animals out of their cages (why the other hens picked on Daisy in the beginning of the story; why the monkeys took the peddler's caps; why the fox never caught Rosie; or whatever)."

49. Encourage children to retell the story — without looking at the pictures. After reading and talking about a familiar storybook with children who have retelling experience, close the book and say something like the following:

"I wonder what parts of the story you can remember without looking at the pictures."

"Let's see if we can tell the story together without looking at the pictures or words, just by remembering it."

Again, this is a challenging task for a person of any age, so support the children's retellings. If a child turns to the book for a reminder, fine. The idea is for children to begin to realize they can carry stories in their minds and imagination wherever they go.

7
Prediction: Imagine a Story's Sequel

At the end of Sam and the Tigers *(Lester), Sari flips back one by one through the pictures of Sam, the main character. "Hmm," she realizes. "Every time, he always wears his old cap." After a pause she speculates, "I bet he's not ever getting a new one 'cause it's his lucky cap!"*

Predicting — that is, thinking ahead, imagining the future — is a habit of mind three- and four-year olds are just developing. As they learn to stretch their minds beyond the immediate moment, they form mental pictures of actions, people, materials, and story characters that are not actually present. Their ability to understand and use both here-and-now language and there-and-then language enables them to become literate (Snow, 1983). The capacity to anticipate and predict allows children to make sense of familiar routines and action sequences in stories they hear and tell. Further, children's growth in comprehension is related to how often they have opportunities to make predictions that cause them to think about the story they are hearing, seeing, and discussing (Dickinson & Smith, 1994).

Young children's story predictions begin in the here-and-now with the observations and comments they make about a character or action on the page open before them. When prompted, they may offer an idea about what they think will appear on the next page. Gradually children begin to make predictions about what will happen next in the story. And with time, experience, and support, they progress to making predictions logically, based on information in the text, the illustrations, or drawn from a related life experience. They may include details and give a reason for a prediction. Children really grasp the idea of prediction when they begin to speculate about a story's sequel, imagining for themselves what a character might do next in a new situation.

Strategies for Prediction

As you read and reread favorite storybooks with children, you can turn to the strategies in this chapter from time to time as ways to vary your joint story-reading interactions. Imagining what might happen next to a story character provides children with another lifelong tool for constructing narrative coherence.

During Story Reading

50. Encourage children to look at and discuss the book's cover and prestory illustrations and speculate what the story might be about. The cover illustration often provides the first clue to the story. It may show the story's characters, pivotal events, or important objects and suggest the overall nature of the tale — for example, something funny, or scary, or about a dog. Covers, like the one for *Sylvester and the Magic Pebble* (Steig), sometimes use an illustration that reappears later in the story. Potentially, as children examine and talk about the cover picture, they begin to formulate ideas about the story's possibilities.

To begin such a conversation, you might say something like the following:

"I wonder what you can tell about this story by looking at the picture on the cover."

"I wonder what the cover tells you about *who* or *what* might be in this story."

"It looks like the donkeys are talking to the pig and chickens. I wonder what they could be talking about."

As you look at the cover of *A Chair for My Mother* (Williams), for example, children might talk about the little girl peering in the window and what she sees inside the blue building; they might figure out that the building is a restaurant or place where people are eating. Noticing these details helps them generate ideas about the story to follow.

You can have similar conversations about the prestory pictures that may appear on the front-matter pages before the story formally begins. These illustrations serve as footprints along a pathway between the cover and the first formal story page. The title page of *Rosie's Walk* (Hutchins), for example, illustrates the entire barnyard where each episode of the story unfolds. To skip over this story map "to get to the story" would deprive children of an engaging reference page they can return to again and again once they know about it!

51. Listen to, acknowledge, and support children's predictions. By doing so, you encourage the habit of thinking ahead and imagining what might happen next. One way to do this is to include children's predictions in your comments. Here are some examples from conversations about *Rosie's Walk* (Hutchins):

Child:	*(Looking at the cover illustration)* He's gonna get her!
You:	It looks like the fox is going to get Rosie!

▼

Child:	*(Points to a rabbit on the title page)* Bunny! By her. *(Points to Rosie)*
You:	There's a bunny by Rosie's house.
Child:	They might be friends.
You:	Maybe the bunny and Rosie are friends.

▼

Child:	*(Looking at a story page)* He's gonna get her now.
You:	It sure looks like the fox is going to get Rosie this time! He's almost on top of her!

Don't worry about correcting children's predictions. The story itself will do that. In the meantime, the children have the satisfaction of working out a number of possibilities for themselves. Remember, it is the act of engaging with and thinking about story events and characters that makes predicting a valuable tool for building story comprehension.

52. After children talk about what they see in an illustration, invite them to anticipate *who* or *what* they might see when they turn the page. Listen to and support children's comments and observations about the picture before them, then say something like "I wonder what we'll see next when we turn the page." As always, pause to listen to and support their ideas. If no one has an idea, you might offer one yourself, for example, "Maybe we'll see Rosie the hen (the man with

Teachers help children build comprehension skills by supporting children's observations about what they see on the current page and encouraging them to think about what they might see on the next page.

his door, the boy with the red jacket, or whomever) again." Or you simply might say, "Let's turn the page and find out." As children gain experience with thinking ahead about something not yet occurring, they will offer more suggestions.

As you look at the next page together, support children's predictions and findings with comments like the following:

> "You thought you might see the girl with the basket (or whatever) on the next page, and here she is!"

> "You predicted you would see lots of chickens on the next page, and you saw one chicken, a dog, and some birds!"

53. Encourage children to listen to the words and anticipate what they might hear more about in the story. After looking at and talking about the illustrations, say something like "Now let's find out what the words tell us about the girl and her chickens (or whomever the characters may be)."

Read the words on each page, pausing to encourage children to talk about the characters they hear about and see. As you read *Daisy Comes Home* (Brett), for example, you might say something like "It says that the hens live in Mei Mei's sandy yard. I wonder who Mei Mei is." After children have speculated about Mei Mei (and perhaps connected her with the girl pictured on the cover), say something like "I wonder if we'll hear about or see Mei Mei (or whomever) on the next page." Continue reading in this manner.

After reading a page and encouraging the child to examine the pictures, this adult supports the child's speculation about what happens on the next page.

On another page, you might say something like "It says that the other hens *crowded* and *jostled* Daisy and *pushed* her off the perch. I wonder what Daisy will do now." After children have talked about Daisy's predicament and speculated about what Daisy might do, say something like "Let's read and find out if Daisy does try to get back on the perch (run away, get in the river, or whatever the children have predicted)."

After reading another page, you might say something like "It says that Mei Mei tries hard to make her hens happy. I wonder if the hens will be happy on the next page of the story." Listen to and support children's thinking about this idea and how it relates to what actually happens on the next page. Continue in this manner to the end of the story.

54. Invite children to predict what a character might *do* next. To shift the focus to actions, say something like "Let's look at the picture on the cover. I wonder what kinds of things you think the girl and the chickens (or whatever is pictured on the cover) might *do* in this story." Listen to and support children's comments and ideas. When the children have had their say, say something like "Let's turn the page and see if the girl and the chickens (or whoever) *are* flying, sleeping, playing, jumping up and down (or whatever actions the children anticipate)."

As you look at and read subsequent pages, you might encourage children to predict actions by making comments and observations like the following:

> "Yes, Mr and Mrs Mallard have been flying a lot. I wonder what they might be doing on the next page."

> "Wow! Sylvester *did* turn into a rock. I wonder what you think he might do now."

> "Yes, Sam has lost all his fine clothes! Now what do you think he might do?"

55. Notice recurring objects and actions and invite children to anticipate their next appearance. Some children's books include objects that appear somewhere in each illustration. While they may or may not have any particular relevance to the main story, they often tell a little side story of their own and provide enjoyable opportunities for prediction.

In *Good Night, Gorilla* (Rathmann), for example, a balloon, released by a mouse in need of its string, floats along on each page as the story progresses. The banana the mouse attaches the string to also gets dragged along through each story episode. With a few initial prompts from you — "I wonder where you think the balloon will go next" or "I wonder how the mouse might move the banana on the next page" — children begin to anticipate, on their own, the appearance of these objects from page to page.

While the peddler's caps in *Caps for Sale* (Slobodkina) play a more pivotal story role than does the balloon or the banana in *Good Night, Gorilla,* they also appear on each page, often in unusual places, and provide ongoing opportunities for prediction.

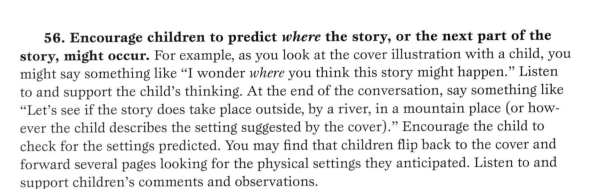

56. Encourage children to predict *where* the story, or the next part of the story, might occur. For example, as you look at the cover illustration with a child, you might say something like "I wonder *where* you think this story might happen." Listen to and support the child's thinking. At the end of the conversation, say something like "Let's see if the story does take place outside, by a river, in a mountain place (or however the child describes the setting suggested by the cover)." Encourage the child to check for the settings predicted. You may find that children flip back to the cover and forward several pages looking for the physical settings they anticipated. Listen to and support children's comments and observations.

As you continue with a story, encourage children to examine and talk about the places they see, predict where the characters on that page will be next, and turn the page(s) so they can check their ideas. Support their findings with comments like the following:

> "You thought Daisy the hen might still be on the river, and she is!"

> "You thought Mei Mei might be at her house, and here she is in a different place, on the sidewalk in the city!"

57. Encourage children to predict *how* something might occur. Whenever a story character faces a particular problem or predicament, children have the opportunity to predict how the character might try to solve the problem. For example, in *Caps for Sale* (Slobodkina), when the peddler looks up and sees that the monkeys in the tree are wearing his caps, you might have a conversation like this one:

You:	I wonder how you think the peddler could get his caps back.
Child:	*(Thinks)* Climb up there and get 'em.
You:	He might climb up the tree after the monkeys and get his caps.
Child:	Or call their mom.
You:	He might call their mom and she would …
Child:	She says to give 'em back.
You:	So he might climb the tree or get their mom to tell them to give the caps back.
Child:	*(Turns the page)* He's shouting!
You:	I wonder if that will work …

When Mr. Gumpy's car gets stuck in *Mr. Gumpy's Motor Car* (Burningham), you might begin a "how" conversation by saying something like "How do you think Mr. Gumpy might get his car out of the mud?" Or when Sal ends up with Little Bear's mother and Little Bear ends up with Sal's mother in *Blueberries for Sal* (McCloskey), you might say, "How do you think Sal and Little Bear might get back to their own moms?"

58. Encourage children to predict a *change* on the next page. When children have examined and talked about a story page, ask them to think and talk about something *new* or *different* they might see on the following page. For example, a conversation about an early illustration in *Daisy Comes Home* (Brett) might begin like this:

You: I wonder what new things you might see in the next picture.

Child: New things?

You: Yes, objects or people or animals you don't see on this page, but that you might see on the next page.

Child: Maybe, maybe eggs!

You: Hmm. You think we might see eggs on the next page.

Child: In that basket. Eggs in that basket …

Support children's thinking about what they find as they flip back and forth to compare illustrations and check their predictions.

59. Encourage children to predict the next part or episode of a story. This strategy encourages children to begin to think ahead about larger chunks of the story. You might begin by saying something like "Something will happen in the first part of the story. I wonder what the cover makes you think it might be." Listen to and support children's thinking and predictions. At the end of the conversation, say something like "Let's look at the pictures in the first part of the story to see if any of these things do happen!"

Mark the end of the first part of the story with a bookmark or sticky note. Then, encourage children to check for the events they predicted as they look through the pictures in that part of the story. Listen to and support children's comments, observations, and thinking.

Next, say something like "Now I wonder what you think is going to happen in the next part of the story." Listen to and support children's thinking about what might happen in the next episode. Then, move the bookmark or sticky note to the end of that episode and encourage children to check and discuss their predictions. Repeat this process through each story episode.

60. Encourage children who have some ease with prediction to look for and talk about clues to what might happen next. To begin, you might say something like "I wonder what clues you think the cover picture gives you about this story." Listen to and support children's thinking about clues to the story they find on the cover. For example, as you read *Daisy Comes Home* (Brett) you might have a conversation like this:

Child 1: This hen is a clue 'cause it's about Daisy.

Child 2: Yeah, Daisy the hen.

Child 1:   And the river. Daisy goes on it.

Child 2:   It's "Daisy Comes Home" and that's what happens!

Child 1:   She goes on it, and then she comes back to her house.

You: So, the hens and the river give you a clue about Daisy the hen going down the river. And the title "Daisy Comes Home" gives you a clue that Daisy comes back home again.

As you look together at each illustration or two-page spread, encourage children to look for clues about what happens next. They may flip forward several pages to connect the clues they see on one page with what happens on a later page. Listen to and support children's observations and thinking. A conversation about a story page might begin something like this:

Child 1:   These hens are mean to Daisy. *(Flips ahead several pages)* And this dog wants to bite her.

Child 2:   Yeah, look. *(Flips ahead)* The man grabs her legs.

Child 1:   He's hurting Daisy!

You: So, the hens' meanness to Daisy is a clue.

Child 1:   Yeah, it's a clue, it's a clue …

You: It is a clue. I'm wondering what it's a clue to.

Child 1:   How there's gonna be, there's gonna be a mean man.

Child 2:   And a mean biting dog!

You: I see. So the hens' meanness to Daisy in this part of the story is a clue to the mean way the dog and the man treat Daisy later on.

After looking for clues in the illustrations, return to the beginning of the story and say something like "Now let's find out what clues the words give us about what might happen next in the story of Daisy (or whomever the story is about)."

Read the words on each page of the first part of the story. Pause often to encourage the children to talk about the situations they hear about and see. Invite children to listen to the words for clues about what might happen next. To encourage conversation about clues in the text, you might say something like this:

"Hmm. Let me read this part again. Maybe there's a clue here.
(Reading) 'Daisy was sleeping and didn't see the river creeping up the bank from all the rain. And when the water reached her Happy Hens basket, she didn't feel it float out into the river.'"

Listen to and support children's thinking about clues they hear about the rain, for example, or the river creeping up the bank. Continue in this manner reading and conversing about clues in each episode to the end of the story.

61. When the story permits, invite children who have some ease with prediction to make predictions about a pair of characters. For example, as you read *Good Night, Gorilla* (Rathmann) with children, you might say something like "Hmm … I wonder what we can find out about the gorilla and the zookeeper from this picture." Give children plenty of time to look and describe what they see both characters doing. Support their observations and wonder aloud about what you'll see these two characters doing on the next page. When the children turn the page, acknowledge their predictions and support their desire to flip back and forth to check their predictions. This focus on the interweaving actions of two characters adds complexity to children's storytelling and prediction.

At The End of the Story

62. Ask children what they think a character might do next after the story in the book ends. After reading with children a story they have looked at and talked about a number of times, invite them to think about what other adventures a character might have or what other things might happen if the story were to continue. Listen to and support their ideas. Children may wish to examine the last page of the book for clues or recall what happened in the story.

For example, after reading and talking about *Rosie's Walk,* you might say, "I wonder what else might happen to Rosie or the fox" or "I wonder what will happen if Rosie takes a walk the next day." A child may offer ideas closely related to those in the book or ideas that lead the story in a new and different direction. No matter what children imagine, support and encourage them to elaborate their ideas. For example, you might respond, "Yes, the fox might fall in a mud puddle. I wonder where the puddle would be and what might make him fall in."

Give children materials so they can draw pictures of what might happen next.

63. After reading and conversing with children about the story, ask what *they* plan to do next. The act of predicting what will happen to a character in or after a story and the act of planning what you will do next both require the same forward thinking — mentally moving out of the here-and-now and projecting yourself into the there-and-then. So it makes great sense to ask a child what he or she plans next now that your story reading together has come to a close. A child's plan might be anything from "Play with Max," to "Go to the block area," to "Draw some more pictures," to "Read this book with you again!" You may also articulate your own plan, such as "I'm going to see what Harmony and Maud are doing at the sand and water table," or "After I read this book with you again, I'm going to look at Kerry and Benji's pirate boat."

References

Anderson, R. C., & Pearson, P. D. (1984). A schema-theoretic overview of basic processes in reading comprehension. In P. D. Pearson, R. Barr, M. Kamil, & P. Mosenthal (Eds.), *Handbook of reading research* (pp. 255–291). New York: Longman.

Biemiller, A. (2001). Teaching vocabulary: Early, direct, and sequential. *American Educator, 25*(1), 24–28, 47.

Bolles, E. B. (1988). *Remembering and forgetting: An inquiry into the nature of memory.* New York: Walker and Company.

Brabham, E. G., & Lynch-Brown, C. (2002). Effects of teachers' reading-aloud styles on vocabulary acquisition and comprehension in students in the early elementary grades. *Journal of Educational Psychology, 94*(3), 465–473.

Bus, A., van Ijzendoorn, M., & Pellegrini, A. (1995). Joint book reading makes for success in learning to read: A meta-analysis on intergenerational transmission of literacy. *Review of Educational Research, 65,* 1–21.

Clark-Stewart, K. A., & Beck, R. J. (1999). Maternal scaffolding and children's narrative retelling of a movie story. *Early Childhood Research Quarterly, 14*(3), 409–434.

Cochran-Smith, M. (1984). *The making of a reader.* Norwood, NJ: Ablex.

Cornell, E. H., Senechal, M., & Bodo, L. S. (1988). Recall of picture books by 3-year-old children: Testing and repetition effects in joint reading activities. *Journal of Educational Psychology, 80*(4), 537–542.

Dickinson, D. K., & Smith, M. W. (1994). Long-term effects of preschool teachers' book readings on low-income children's vocabulary and story comprehension. *Reading Research Quarterly, 29,* 104–122.

Duff, A. (1944). *"Bequest of wings": A family's pleasures with books.* New York: Viking Press.

Feagans, L. (1984). Developmental differences in the comprehension and production of narratives by reading-disabled and normally developing children. *Reading Development, 55,* 1727–1736.

Hart, B., & Risley, T. (1999). *The social world of children learning to talk.* Baltimore: Brookes.

Hutchins, P. (1968/1986). *Rosie's walk.* New York: Simon & Schuster.

McKeown, M. G., & Beck, I. L. (2006). Encouraging young children's language interactions with stories. In D. K. Dickinson & S. B. Neuman (Eds.), *Handbook of early literacy research: Vol. 2* (pp. 281–294). New York: Guilford Press.

Morrow, L. M. (1992). The impact of a literature-based program on literacy achievement, use of literature, and attitudes of children from minority backgrounds. *Reading Research Quarterly, 27,* 250–275.

Nagy, W. E., & Scott, J. A. (2000). Vocabulary processes. In M. L. Kamil, P. B. Mosenthal, D. Pearson, & R. Barr (Eds.), *Handbook of reading research: Vol. III* (pp. 269–284). Mahwah, NJ: Lawrence Erlbaum.

Paris, A. H., & Paris, S. G. (2001). *Children's comprehension of narrative picture books.* (CIERA Report #3-012). Ann Arbor, MI: Center for the Improvement of Early Reading Achievement.

Paris, A. H., & Paris, S. G. (2003). Assessing narrative comprehension in young children. *Reading Research Quarterly, 38*(1), 36–76.

Paris, S. G. (2004, July). *How to teach and assess reading comprehension.* PowerPoint presentation, CIERA Summer Institute, Center for the Improvement of Early Reading Achievement, Ann Arbor, MI.

Roth, F. P. (1986). Oral narrative abilities of learning-disabled students. *Topics in Language Disorder, 7,* 21–30.

Seuling, B. (2007, June). How to refine your picture book. *The Writer, 20*(6), 28–40.

Shank, R. (1990). *Tell me a story: A new look at real and artificial memory.* New York: Scribners.

Slobodkina, E. 1947/1987. *Caps for sale.* Reading, MA: Addison-Wesley.

Snow, C. E. (1983). Literacy and language: Relationships during the preschool years. *Harvard Educational Review, 53,* 165–189.

Snow, C. E., Tabors, P. O., & Dickinson, D. K. (2001). Language development in the preschool years. In D. K. Dickinson & P. O. Tabors (Eds.), *Beginning literacy with language: Young children learning at home and school* (pp. 1–25). Baltimore: Paul H. Brookes Publishing Co.

Snow, C. E., Tabors, P. O., Nicholson, P. A., & Kurland, B. F. (1995). SHELL: Oral language and literacy skills in kindergarten and first-grade children. *Journal of Research in Childhood Education, 10,* 37–47.

Sulzby, E. (1985). Children's emergent reading of favorite storybooks: A developmental study. *Reading Research Quarterly, 20*(4), 458–481.

Sulzby, E., & Barnhart, J. (1990). The developing kindergartener: All our children emerge as writers and readers. In J. S. McKee (Ed.), *The developing kindergarten: Programs, children, & teachers* (pp. 201–224). Ann Arbor: Michigan Association for the Education of Young Children (MiAEYC).

Sulzby, E., & Rockafellow, B. (2001). *Sulzby Classification Scheme instructional profiles.* Ann Arbor: Sulzby Classification Scheme/Michigan Literacy Progress Profile (SCS/MLPP).

Teale, W. H. (2003). Reading aloud to young children as a classroom instructional activity: Insights from research and practice. In A. van Kleeck, A. S. Stahl, & E. B. Bauer (Eds.), *On reading books to children* (pp. 114–139). Mahwah, NJ: Erlbaum.

Teale, W. H., & Martinez, M. G. (1996). Reading aloud to young children: Teachers' reading styles and kindergarteners' text comprehension. In C. Pontecorvo, M. Orsolini, B. Burge, & L. Resnick (Eds.), *Children's early text construction* (pp. 321–344). Mahwah, NJ: Erbaum.

Whitehurst, G. J., Falco, F., Lonigan, C. J., Fischel, J., DeBaryshe, B., Valdez-Menchaca, M., & Caulfield, M. (1988). Accelerating language development through picture-book reading. *Developmental Psychology, 24,* 552–558.

Appendix: Master List of Strategies

The following is a master list of the strategies for interactive storybook reading given in Chapters 3–7:

1. Read with individual and small groups of children.

2. Take a leisurely approach to story reading and book talk.

3. Encourage children to engage physically with the book itself.

4. Start with the pictures, then move to the text.

5. Have children do the lion's share of the talking.

6. Listen to children — with interest.

7. Elicit and respond to children's comments and observations.

8. Ask open-ended questions from time to time.

9. Answer children's questions.

10. Support children's ideas.

11. Think aloud about the story from time to time.

12. Create opportunities for children to think about the story.

13. Flip back and forth in the story as needed.

14. Read a book many times with children.

15. Look for unusual words in the text.

16. Attune yourself to the words offered by the pictures.

17. Invite children to talk about what they see in pictures.

18. Incorporate some of the book's vocabulary into your own comments and observations.

19. Use synonyms, definitions, and root words.

20. Look up words in the dictionary with children.

21. Connect words to children's gestures and emerging ideas.

22. Encourage children to try out action words they see in pictures and hear in text.

23. Draw children's attention to the vocabulary of design.

24. Encourage children to look for and talk about recurring design features.

25. Use words and phrases from stories in your everyday conversations with children.

26. Encourage children to talk about objects, animals, and people they see in illustrations on the cover and pages of the book.

27. Converse with children about things in pictures they have seen or played with themselves.

28. Encourage children to make connections between what they see in the pictures and hear about in the text.

29. Encourage children to comment on *actions* they see and hear about in the story.

30. Encourage children to relate actions in stories to their own actions.

31. Identify recurring characters, objects, and actions with children.

32. Encourage children to figure out *where* an action or scene is happening.

33. Draw children's attention to critical parts or episodes of the story.

34. Look at and read the story episode by episode.

35. Look for and talk about *emotions* depicted in pictures and text.

36. Encourage children to talk about *ideas* they see and hear about in a story.

37. Encourage children to invent words or dialogue for characters in a particular illustration or situation.

38. Ask children to tell *why* they think something happens in the story.

39. Support children's new ideas, connections, and changing understanding of the story over time.

40. Play "I Spy."

41. Refer to the book's cover illustration from time to time.

42. As you look at, read, and talk about a story, pause from time to time for children to recall where in the story they have seen or heard about the same characters, objects, or actions.

43. Pause from time to time to encourage children to recall an earlier part of the story.

44. Encourage children to find an illustration they particularly like and retell that part of the story.

45. Consider using storyboards to encourage retelling.

46. From time to time, encourage children to recall and draw, model, or reenact something they liked from the story.

47. Wonder out loud about *changes* that occur in the story, and listen to children's ideas.

48. Wonder out loud *why* story events unfold as they do and listen to children's ideas.

49. Encourage children to retell the story — without looking at the pictures.

50. Encourage children to look at and discuss the book's cover and prestory illustrations and speculate what the story might be about.

51. Listen to, acknowledge, and support children's predictions.

52. After children talk about what they see in an illustration, invite them to anticipate *who* or *what* they might see when they turn the page.

53. Encourage children to listen to the words and anticipate what they might hear more about in the story.

54. Invite children to predict what a character might *do* next.

55. Notice recurring objects and actions and invite children to anticipate their next appearance.

56. Encourage children to predict *where* the story, or the next part of the story, might occur.

57. Encourage children to predict *how* something might occur.

58. Encourage children to predict a *change* on the next page.

59. Encourage children to predict the next part or episode of a story.

60. Encourage children who have some ease with prediction to look for and talk about clues to what might happen next.

61. When the story permits, invite children who have some ease with prediction to make predictions about a pair of characters.

62. Ask children what they think a character might do next after the story in the book ends.

63. After reading and conversing with children about the story, ask what *they* plan to do next.

Index

About the Authors

Mary Hohmann, retired HighScope senior early childhood specialist, was a member of the HighScope Educational Research Foundation from 1970–2007. There she served

as a preschool teacher, trainer, curriculum developer, and writer, and as an educational consultant in the United States, Norway, Finland, and Portugal. She is the principal author of the book *Educating Young Children: Active Learning Practices for Preschool and Child Care Programs* and coauthor of the books *Letter Links: Alphabet Learning With Children's Names* and *Tender Care and Early Learning: Supporting Infants and Toddlers in Child Care Settings* — all from the HighScope Press. She is also the author of *Fee, Fie, Phonemic Awareness: 130 Prereading Activities for Preschoolers* and coeditor of *Let's Talk Literacy: Practical Readings for Preschool Teachers,* both from the HighScope Press. Hohmann is one of the developers of the Growing Readers Early Literacy Curriculum and of two early childhood assessment tools, the Preschool Child Observation Record and the Infant-Toddler Child Observation Record.

Kate Adams was an editor/writer at HighScope Educational Research Foundation from 2004–2005, where she worked with Mary Hohmann on the Growing Readers Early Literacy Curriculum. Before joining HighScope, Kate taught English language learners in Chicago's Ukrainian Village and worked as an editor for World Book Encyclopedia. She now edits educational textbooks for elementary students.